More Praise for *The Practicing Mind*

"Thomas Sterner's book has provided helpful information in all areas of my life. As a business leader, I became more effective; as a public speaker, more dynamic; as a parent, more attentive; and with my weekend hobbies, I learned to have more fun and increase skills. *The Practicing Mind* helped me realize that the way to get to an end was just as important as the end, if not more so. Life is a journey and not a destination; thanks to Mr. Sterner, I love the journey."

— Ralph Citino, banking professional

"*The Practicing Mind* engagingly transforms difficulty into devotion, offering a practical, easy-to-understand approach that will transform your view of even the most challenging or mundane steps on your journey of life. In clear language and interesting personal anecdotes, Thomas Sterner shows us that by mindfully focusing on the *process* of pursuing our goals, we can let go of attachments to the outcomes we cannot control. So much suffering in our modern world could be alleviated if everyone absorbed Sterner's very wise lessons."

— Marney K. Makridakis, author of *Creating Time* and founder of ArtellaLand.com

"In *The Practicing Mind*, Tom Sterner achieves a rare combination: he provides not just a clear set of practical steps for creating focused effort but also a theoretical background that can help us to reframe our expectations and values so that we can keep in perspective the difference between process and product, progress and goals. Highly recommended."

— Dr. Scott A. Davison, professor of philosophy at Morehead State University and author of *On the Intrinsic Value of Everything*

"Thomas Sterner elucidates a paradox of life: real achievement requires patience and discipline, and in order to develop these qualities one must apply both of them. He then guides us, with many practical examples from his own experience, to resolve this paradox through the application of mindfulness. Sterner shows us how to be present, how to observe without judging, and in the process, we liberate our natural ability to learn. Paradoxically, as you embrace the process-oriented approach described in *The Practicing Mind*, you'll achieve better results in any endeavor."

— Michael J. Gelb, author of
How to Think Like Leonardo da Vinci
and *Brain Power: Improve Your Mind as You Age*

"In a society of immediate gratification, Thomas M. Sterner's book *The Practicing Mind* almost parodies itself. Designed to be a primer for slowing down, becoming more aware of the present moment, and increasing self-discipline and focus, Sterner's brilliance shines through in the brevity of this complex book's pages.... [T]his tiny but intense book delivers enough information to contemplate and apply for a lifetime."

— *Roundtable Reviews*

The

PRACTICING MIND

The

PRACTICING MIND

Developing Focus and Discipline in Your Life

THOMAS M. STERNER

New World Library
Novato, California

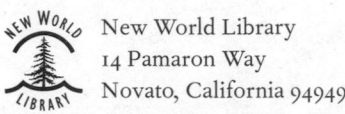

New World Library
14 Pamaron Way
Novato, California 94949

Originally published by Mountain Sage Publishing in 2005

Text design by Tona Pearce Myers

Library of Congress Cataloging-in-Publication Data
Sterner, Thomas M., date.
 The practicing mind : developing focus and discipline in your life : master any skill or challenge by learning to love the process / Thomas M. Sterner. — 1st ed.
    p.   cm.
Includes index.
ISBN 978-1-60868-090-0 (pbk. : alk. paper)
1. Mind and body. 2. Persistence. 3. Self-control. I. Title.
BF151.S74 2012
153.1'534—dc23   2011050865

First New World Library edition, April 2012
ISBN 978-1-60868-090-0
Printed in Canada on 100% postconsumer-waste recycled paper

New World Library is proud to be a Gold Certified Environmentally Responsible Publisher. Publisher certification awarded by Green Press Initiative. www.greenpressinitiative.org

10 9 8 7 6

*This book is dedicated
to the gentle spirit of my mother,
Margaret Sterner.
You taught so many, so much,
with so few words.*

Contents

Acknowledgments

I would like to thank the people who made this book possible.

To my wife, Jamie, and my two daughters, Margie and Melissa, I say thank you for believing in me and being patient with the long process of getting here.

To my father, I must say thank you for a lifetime of support and friendship beyond any words.

Finally, to my close friend and editor (perhaps an unusual combination) Lin Bloom McDowell, thank you for helping me to say what I needed and wanted to say. Editors are the invisible heroes who make creating a book possible.

Introduction

Real peace and contentment in our lives come from realizing that life is a process to engage in, a journey down a path that we can choose to experience as magical.

The Practicing Mind is about remembering what you already know at some level and bringing that memory into the present, where it will both serve to place you on that path and empower you to partake in the journey. This book will reintroduce you to a process you followed to acquire a skill before you knew what *process* meant, and it will remind you that life itself is nothing more than one long practice session, an endless effort to refine the motions, both physical and mental, that compose our days.

We all understand that activities such as learning to play a musical instrument and developing a fundamentally sound golf swing are skills and as such require practice. But in fact, life is a journey that requires and even forces us — either consciously or unconsciously — to master one skill after another. We easily forget that when our lives here began, learning to walk and to articulate our thoughts and feelings started from a place of "no skill." Driven by both desire and necessity, we mastered these skills one step at a time, one sound at a time, and, perhaps most important, without a sense of struggle. Just as with such endeavors as music or golf, we acquired these skills by the process we call *practice*: the repetition of an activity with the purposeful awareness and intention of accomplishing an intended goal.

In our overpaced and overstressed world today, we use the word *skill* to define a personal asset; for example, we might say, "That is not part of my skill set." At the same time, our recognition of the value of possessing many diverse skills is expanding. Ironically, though, we miss the point that the ability to develop any skill as swiftly as possible, with the least amount of effort, and even to experience inner peace and joy in the process, is in fact a skill itself, and one that requires constant practice to become an effortless part of who we are.

When we learn to focus on and embrace the process of experiencing life, whether we're working toward a personal aspiration or working through a difficult time, we begin to free ourselves from the stress and anxiety that are born out of our attachment to our goals, our sense that "I can't feel happiness until I *reach* my goal." This "goal" always takes the form of someplace we have not yet reached, something we don't yet have but will at some point, and then, we believe, all will be right in our life.

When we subtly shift toward both focusing on and finding joy in the process of *achieving* instead of *having* the goal, we have gained a new skill. And once mastered, it is magical and incredibly empowering.

We describe those who demonstrate this "skill" as possessing such qualities as self-discipline, focus, patience, and self-awareness, and we recognize that these all-important virtues are interwoven threads in the fabric of true inner peace and contentment in life. With this skill, we are masters of the energy we expend in life, and without it, we are victims of our own unfocused and constantly changing efforts, desires, and directions.

The Practicing Mind helps you to understand and develop this skill as a natural part of who you are, and to understand how the culture we live in constantly instructs us to the contrary. This book is about how learning to live in the present moment and becoming process-oriented centers us on this magical path and brings us a wonderful sense of patience with both ourselves and our lives as we learn to enjoy our journey.

*Everything in life worth achieving
requires practice. In fact,
life itself is nothing more than one
long practice session, an endless effort
of refining our motions. When the proper
mechanics of practice are understood,
the task of learning something new becomes
a stress-free experience of joy and calmness,
a process which settles all areas in your life
and promotes proper perspective
on all of life's difficulties.*

CHAPTER 1

The Learning Begins

When I was a child, I studied the guitar, though I was so young at the time (just four years old) that I don't remember much of it. However, as I look back on the music I played, it's fair to say that I acquired a substantial amount of skill. Yet I quit after two years and did nothing much, musically speaking, for the next several years. At the age of nine, like so many kids growing up, I began studying the piano. Once again, this lasted briefly, this time only ten months, and the reason for this was that I really didn't enjoy practicing. If asked why, I probably would have said that it was boring and difficult, and that I felt as if I wasn't getting any better. Though my perspective may have been accurate at the time, it stemmed from the fact that I wasn't very good at the process of practicing music, or practicing anything else, for that matter. Unfortunately, I was far from sophisticated enough to realize this. However, because of my love for music, I eventually returned to the piano and did go on to learn to play.

During my late teens and early twenties, when I was still single, I pursued music very seriously and achieved a fair amount of success. I could compose and arrange in just about any style. I played as a professional in many settings, from the nicest country clubs to the worst taprooms. I put together a rather expensive recording studio and became acquainted with some of the better-known songwriters and artists in the worlds of pop, jazz, and country. By the time I hit my midtwenties, I was a pretty good musician by most people's standards.

My musical development continued, and by the time I reached my midthirties, I began to realize that something had really changed in me with regard to my feelings toward practicing. I not only loved to practice and learn anything but found the total immersion of myself into an activity to be an escape from the daily pressures of life. I even felt cheated if I was deprived of an opportunity to practice something, such as a particular aspect of my golf swing. Much more important, I was beginning to understand that all of life is practice, in one form or another. Until then, like most people, I mistakenly associated the word *practice* only with art forms such as music, dance, and painting. I did not see dealing with a cranky child, an overburdened work schedule, or a tight monthly budget as actions that required applying the same principles as learning music did.

As my comprehension of the relationship among life, mental discipline, and practice grew, I began to direct all my effort into defining the fundamentals of the *practicing mind*, and into observing when and how often I applied these fundamentals in daily living. I wanted to better understand the changes in my perspective that had created such a turnaround in my attitudes toward the process of learning something new. Had I just grown up and matured, or was something more defined, something more tangible, developing in my mind? I knew I processed life differently than I had in the past, but what were the mechanics of the new system? That was what I needed to know.

I didn't realize at the time that it was my experience of learning music growing up that had laid the foundation that would help me understand both the mental and spiritual struggles in which I now found myself as I searched for answers. Those early experiences — of wanting to accomplish something while dealing with a personality that was not particularly well disciplined at the time — went a long way toward helping me understand why we fail at endeavors that might be very important to us. My successes and failures in music provided me with a point of reference to which I constantly compared my daily experiences. That is why you will see references to music throughout this book. It is not, however, necessary that you yourself have studied music to feel a kinship with me as I describe the aspects of music that taught me so much. Since the nature of the practicing mind exists in all activities of life, you will, no doubt, be able to relate my experiences to those that you have had in your own life.

As important as music was to my learning process, it

wasn't the activity that first inspired change in how I approached daily life. Instead, I first became aware of the shift in my perspective toward practicing when, on my wife's advice, I took up golf in my early thirties. I think, initially, the reason I didn't see my early days of musical study as being a backdrop for this change in awareness was because those experiences were so far removed from the present day. Indeed, by this time in my life, music was second nature to me, and my practice regimen was so natural that I no longer had the perspective of a struggling student. Golf, on the other hand, was totally new to me. I knew almost nothing about it, and I had no preconceived ideas of how it should be played.

In the beginning, my father-in-law would take me out to play on his course, and I would rent or borrow some old clubs. I quickly experienced the frustrations of the game, but what made a bigger impression on me was that I didn't see anybody playing who was really any good. Most of the people I observed had been playing golf for as long as I had been playing piano, and yet in their own activity they hadn't gotten out of book one, so to speak. They played terribly and seemed clueless about how to fix their problems with the game.

What I mean is that even though they had played golf weekly for many years, they still couldn't accomplish basic things, such as getting the ball up in the air. They couldn't hit the ball where they were aiming, they never improved, and they had no idea why. By that time, they should have been able not only to hit the ball hundreds of yards at their target but also to do things like make the ball go high or low and curve its flight from right to left at will. Armed with their total lack of knowledge of how they *should* swing the golf club, or what they actually looked like when they did, they were repeating the same lack of fundamental skills over and over again and expecting different results. To compare this to music, it would be like watching someone who had been playing the piano for twenty years get frustrated at his inability to play more than one note at a time because he didn't realize he was supposed to play with his fingers, not his elbows.

Perhaps my biggest advantage was that, even though I was not uncoordinated, I had not excelled in any sports growing up. Therefore, I assumed I would need to find an instructor to guide my learning process, lest I end up like so many other eternally frustrated golfers. Also, because I had grown up trying to learn to play musical instruments (besides guitar and piano, I also studied the flute and saxophone), I *expected* that mastering the skills that would bring both consistency and joy to the game would take time and applied effort. It never occurred to me that golf would be a quick or easy study. I was undaunted by, but yet aware of, the fact that despite my ability to play the piano well, I had fallen short of many of my musical goals. I comforted myself with my knowledge that I was an adult now, armed with an adult mentality and all that I had learned from those failures. I was sure this would see me through to achieving my goals in this newfound endeavor.

What I learned from golf was that all my failures in music had stemmed from my lack of understanding the proper mechanics of practicing, of the process of picking a goal, whatever that may be, and applying a steady effort toward achieving it. Perhaps most important, I realized that I had learned how to accomplish just that *without* the frustration and anxiety usually associated with such an activity.

Golf provided me with my first opportunity to quantify these mechanics into something tangible to someone with my upbringing; before this point, I was like everyone who had come before me. I wanted the joy and benefits that are rewarded to the individual who perseveres at working toward a lofty personal goal. I wanted to experience the self-discovery that one attains by picking a goal and steadily working toward it, regardless of the pitfalls and frustration. This desire to learn is only the first step, though. Without an understanding of proper practice mechanics, and without an awareness of our own internal workings, we're almost certain to use up the initial inspiration and motivation that propelled us into our endeavor, leaving us feeling we cannot reach the goal that had seemed so worth striving for just a short time earlier.

Why bother with any of this? This is a question I asked myself. I mean, really, what is the relevance of this to how we live our lives day to day? How does understanding and developing this mindset impact what we experience moment by moment, what we accomplish, and who we are? The answer is that this mindset influences everything. It is the blank page on which we draw our lives. It determines not only what we draw but also what we are *able* to draw. It shapes every aspect of who we are, what we become, and how we see others. It is self-discipline and self-awareness. It gives us patience with ourselves, with others, and with life itself. It is certainly one of the most powerful and meaningful gifts we can give ourselves — and yes, only *we* can give this gift to ourselves.

Our culture today is one built on multitasking. Multitasking is emphasized not just to increase productivity (which never seems to be enough), but for survival. We teach it to ourselves, and we teach it to our children. We are always doing and thinking of more than one thing at a time.

Think about the simple act of driving a car. What is the first thing many of us do after we start the car? We turn on the radio. Now we are driving *and* listening to the radio. If someone is with us, we are carrying on a conversation on top of that. If we are alone, we might talk on a cell phone. Our minds are juggling many activities, and our energies are very dispersed. Even though this tires us completely, it has become normal for us as our world moves faster and faster. We don't even question the levels of absurdity that multitasking reaches at times.

Years ago, I took one of my daughters to a skating party sponsored by the sixth grade of her school. I told her I would sit inconspicuously in the concession area and read while she skated. Here is what I saw and heard as I observed the scene. Six TV monitors hung from the ceiling along the main side of the rink, where people put on their skates. Each TV played a different channel, and each one's volume competed with those of all the other TVs. Loud music was playing throughout the rink. There was a video-game area where about a half-dozen full-size arcade machines blared out their own sound effects. There was also a seven-foot TV screen at one end of the rink playing a music video that was different than the music playing on the house PA system. Finally, there were all these eleven-year-old kids skating around the rink, and none of them were talking to one another. How could they? Just skating while absorbing all this sensory input that the mind needed to process was exhausting.

At times we must do several things at once, but the problem for us is that we are so used to always multitasking that when we decide we want to reel in our minds and focus ourselves on just one activity, we can't. Our minds are so agitated, and that agitation has a tremendous amount of momentum. It doesn't want to stop moving. It tires us out and stresses us out. We find we can't sit still, and we can't *be* still. However, the practicing mind is quiet. It lives in the present and has laser-like, pinpoint focus and accuracy. It obeys our precise directions, and all our energy moves through it. Because of this, we are calm and completely free of anxiety. We are where we should be at that moment, doing what we should be doing and completely aware of what we are experiencing. There is no wasted motion, physically or mentally.

Going back to the car example, how many times have

you driven somewhere and then noticed that you didn't remember a portion of the ride? The reason you experience this is because instead of focusing on driving the car, your mind was overflowing with unrelated thoughts. So few people are really aware of their thoughts. Their minds run all over the place without their permission, and they go along for the ride unknowingly and without making a choice. Instead of observing their thoughts and using their thoughts to serve themselves, they are *in* their thoughts.

If this weren't so tragic, it would be amusing. We are convinced that because our technology is evolving, we must be evolving, too. We think that because we have cell phones with cameras in them, we must be more advanced than people who lived twenty-five hundred years ago; but in fact, those people in the past were much more aware of their internal world than we are because they weren't distracted by technology. We have all this technology, which is supposed to make our lives easier, yet it doesn't. They had none of the technology, but they had much simpler lives and perhaps a better understanding of how their minds worked.

We think that our struggles today are known only to us, but they are timeless, and those who lived long before us faced the same internal struggles that we do. There is a story, many centuries old, that describes these struggles. The story is about a chariot rider who steps onto a Roman-style chariot drawn by four horses. In this story, the horses represent the mind. The driver, who has an undisciplined mind, steps onto the chariot but has no hold on the reins. The four horses run wild all day, exhausting themselves and the driver as they bump along off the chosen path, constantly changing directions. They do not know where they are or where they are going at any given moment. The driver holds on to the railings and is just as helpless as the horses as they all watch the scenery go by. In contrast, a disciplined driver, who has the reins in hand, is in control and directs the horses down the focused, chosen path, wherever it might be. The horses now have no will. Their energy is directed by the refined commands of the disciplined driver. The ride is smooth, and they all reach their desired destination in the least amount of time, with the least amount of effort and fatigue. Which would you rather be?

If you are not in control of your thoughts, then you are not in control of yourself. Without self-control, you have no *real* power, regardless of whatever else you accomplish. If you are not *aware* of the thoughts that you think in each moment, then you are the rider with no reins, with no power over where you are going. You cannot control what you are not aware of. Awareness must come first.

The quest of this book is to examine how we get from here to there. How did we learn to be the chariot driver with no hold on the reins, and what types of cultural habits or teachings reinforce and perpetuate that way of thinking? What can we learn from how kids think? What can we teach them so they will have less to unlearn than we do? How do we do all this without struggling to accomplish it? These are the questions I asked myself, and they are the ones I will, I hope, answer for you.

When I began this project, I envisioned this to be a book that would simply help readers to eliminate the struggles of learning to play a musical instrument. However, the further into the writing process I got, the more I realized that I was writing about my outlook on processing life, not just my thoughts about playing an instrument or learning a golf swing. I realized that I was using what I had learned in the very process of writing the book. I observed my perspective on how I maintained my steady writing effort day to day. I saw its presence in the effort of trying to understand exactly what it was that I had learned and how to put that into words. I saw how I was able to run a very successful business and to be there for my young daughters.

One day, I noticed that I was feeling frustrated and somewhat irritated while I was taking care of my daughters. I was having all these ideas for this book, but they were going to have to wait to be written down because my children needed my attention. I noticed that I had become the chariot driver who did not have control of the reins. I was allowing my mind to run off the path and work on the book instead of staying on the path and enjoying the time with my kids. When I realized this, I pulled in the reins and let the book go until my next scheduled writing session. The stress disappeared immediately, and I dove into the fun I had missed by not being in the present moment with my daughters.

At its inception, I would not have been able to write "this" version of *The Practicing Mind* even if someone had sat me down and said, "I will pay your bills and look after your family. You just write." It took the writing process and observing myself going through my days to learn that.

I now realize that my approach toward moving through life began to change in my early twenties. Maybe this sounds familiar to you. Up until then, I had a long list of interests that I pursued with a lot of enthusiasm at first, and then lost steam and energy relatively quickly. First I would pick a particular activity, say exercising. Then I would really get involved in it by joining a gym, buying the proper clothes, and so forth. Next I would start the activity with a commitment to be steadfast, and I'd persevere in my effort. After a few sessions, my initial enthusiasm would start to taper off, and I would have trouble maintaining my interest and discipline. From that point, it would become harder and harder to continue with the practice of keeping up the exercising routine, and I would begin to make excuses to myself for skipping a session with promises like, "I will make it up in the next session or add one in the morning before work during the week." This was all folly, though, because I wouldn't follow through with these commitments either, and I would become more and more comfortable with letting things slide until I had completely gotten away from my original goals. There was also this nagging sense that I had let myself down, plus a feeling that I was not really in control of my destiny because I wasn't completing something that I had made a decision to do. Eventually, I would get to the point in this cycle where I lost all interest in the particular endeavor, and I would begin the search for the next thing that was going to fill the void in me, starting the whole process over again. My biggest asset was that I was aware of the fact that I followed this cycle when tackling any new endeavor. I noted this tendency, and I would quietly observe myself participating in this routine with one thing after another.

Three things were happening at this point in my life that would prove to be the beginning of a major shift in perspective and awareness for me. First, I had begun taking piano lessons again, from a teacher who not only was one of the best players in the area but was just several years older than me. Taking lessons as an adult yielded a whole new set of advantages and disadvantages over studying as a child. We will go into these in a later chapter. Second, while in college, I had begun independently studying Eastern philosophies. My study at that point was fairly broad, not focusing on any philosophy in particular, and it was part of a self-taught "religions and philosophies of the world" course. It sparked a contemplative process that, over the next twenty years, would forever change my understanding of the relationship between the mechanics of and the reasons for practicing anything.

If you have never considered it, think about how everything we learn and master in life, from walking and tying our shoes to saving money and raising a child, is accomplished through a form of practice, something we repeat over and over again. For the most part, we are not aware of the process as such, but that is how good practice manifests itself when done properly. It carries no stress-laden anticipation, no internal question, "When will the goal be reached?" When we practice anything properly, the fact that we are engaging in a difficult learning process disappears, and, more important, the process dissolves into a period of inner calming that gives us a rest from the tension and anxiety that our "get it done yesterday" world pushes on us every day of our lives. For this reason, it is important to recognize and be in control of the process and to learn to enjoy that part of life's activity.

The third major influence on my shift in perspective toward learning anything new came from a career decision. I had decided to become a concert piano technician and piano rebuilder. This is a very unique vocation, to put it mildly. It takes years to learn the skills necessary to be a high-level concert technician, and even longer to become proficient at the art of fine instrument restoration. My days consisted of anything from preparing a $100,000 concert grand piano for a major world symphony performance to painstakingly restoring a vintage grand piano to better-than-factory-new condition. During my years in business, I worked for and met many of the world's best conductors, concert pianists, big band leaders, and pop, jazz, and country-western singers, and I restored pianos dating back to the Civil War period.

A grand piano action (which is the entire keyboard

mechanism) consists of 8,000 to 10,000 parts. There are 88 notes, with about 34 different adjustments per note. A piano has between 225 and 235 strings, each of which has a corresponding tuning pin that needs to be individually adjusted at least once during a single tuning. My point is obvious. Working on a piano is repetitious, tedious, and monotonous, to say the least. Everything you do to the instrument, you must do at least 88 times. This forces you to let go of everything but the most practical and efficient attitude toward the daily work that faces you in the shop and on the stage. If you do not possess at least a minimal level of discipline and patience, your anxiety and frustration will soar.

My purpose in detailing the repetitive nature and monotony of this work is to give you an appreciation of why, out of sheer survival, I began to develop an ability to get lost in the *process* of doing something. As difficult as the job was, its monotonous nature enabled me to spend my day alone with my thoughts. This afforded me the time to observe and evaluate what worked and what didn't when coping with the nature of my trade.

Throughout this book, I will relate what I consider the key events and areas of my life that taught me so much about myself, why I struggled at times, why I let myself down at times, and how I moved beyond those failures simply by observing some of life's simple truths.

And so, on to the beginning of understanding our *practicing mind*.

A paradox of life:
The problem with patience and discipline
is that developing each of them requires
both of them.

CHAPTER 2

Process, Not Product

During the time I studied golf, I participated in a six-week group golf class. Each week, five of us, all adults, would meet at the driving range for an hour of instruction followed by an hour of practice on our own. At the beginning of the third session, I was sitting on a bench waiting for the class ahead of ours to finish. Next to me was one of my classmates, who had also gotten there early. I had learned, when we had introduced ourselves on the first day, that she was heavily involved in the corporate routine and wanted to learn golf both for relaxation and as a means to further her career. She explained that many times in the course of her job, golf outings were offered as a way to meet new business contacts and discuss company matters in a relaxed setting.

As we chatted about golf and our jobs, I asked her this question: "Well, did you practice what we learned last week?" "No," she replied. "I had so much to do all week. I just want to wake up one morning and be able to play well." I sensed frustration and mild depression in her voice. She seemed frustrated that golf was much harder than it looked and depressed about all the hard work that lay ahead of her if she had any hopes of reaching the level of ability that she felt would make the game more fun.

When our class began, the instructor asked that same question of all of us, even though he would know the truth as soon as we started warming up and hitting balls. The purpose of his question was to make us admit, out loud, whether or not we had found the discipline necessary to practice and habitualize the techniques that he had taught to us the previous week. *That* would allow us to easily move on to the next step. What was revealed was that only two of us had practiced at all during the week between sessions. One classmate had been to the range several evenings to go over what he had been shown. The remaining three not only had failed to practice but had left immediately after the instruction period the week before instead of remaining to practice on their own. My weekly practice included the following:

After class the previous Monday evening, I had stayed and hit balls for an hour to begin learning what had been shown to us during the lesson. Before leaving the range, I sat in the car and spent a few minutes writing down notes in a small journal. I made sure that I wrote a description of everything we had covered in class. These notes were nothing elaborate, just reminders of the key points the instructor had discussed. During the week that followed, I would go into my basement to practice after my children had gone to bed and my wife and I had caught up on each other's day. I made a list of everything I would cover in that particular practice session, and divided up each task so that I could work on only one aspect of the golf swing at a time. In the course of practicing each item, I would make anywhere from one to two hundred swings in front of a mirror with a short club I had cut off so it wouldn't hit the ceiling. I followed this up during the week with three trips to the range to actually hit balls, but again, only working on one part of the swing at a time. When at the range, I put most of my energy into ignoring what the ball flight looked like. I was in the *process* of learning parts of the golf swing. I didn't expect to be hitting good shots. A beautiful golf shot is the result, or *product*, of all the parts being correct.

To my classmates, this type of practice routine would seem to require way too much time and effort out of their already overburdened days. However, the reality was that, just as in learning a musical instrument as a child, I rarely put in more than an hour of practice time a day. Just turning the TV off would give the average person much more time than was required. More important, I not only looked forward to the practice sessions but *needed* them. They provided me with a diversion.

Just as for everyone else, my life was stressful at times, and I anticipated absorbing myself in something that *wasn't.* Besides the normal ups and downs of family life, I had career deadlines to meet: expensive piano restoration work that clients had saved years for and wanted finished on time, regardless of whether some supplier had sent me the wrong parts or I had lost time to emergency service work for a symphony. I also had to deal with nerve-wracking concert situations while preparing pianos for some of the biggest names in the music world. If there was a problem, I was the "go-to" man. I had to provide the solution right now, and no excuses. At more than one symphonic concert, I found myself frantically searching for some perceived nuance of imperfection while the artist looked over my shoulder and a thousand people were kept waiting in the lobby for us to finish and clear the stage. Stress was no stranger to my job experience.

Contrary to what the other classmates were experiencing, I found that, when given my *present-moment* attention, the practice sessions were very calming, not bothersome. I didn't have to be anywhere but "here," and I didn't have to accomplish anything but exactly what I was doing "right now." I found that immersing myself in the process of practicing shut off all the tensions of the day and all the thoughts of what had to get done tomorrow. It kept my mind in the present, out of the past and the future. I let go of any expectations about how long it would take me to acquire a good golf swing because I was enjoying what I was doing right now: learning a good golf swing.

Why was I finding golf practice to be an invigorating yet calming experience while my classmates were finding it to be the opposite? I believe this was because I was actually practicing and they were not. Compounding the problem was their anxiety, which was created by their awareness that by not practicing, they were not getting any closer to their intended goal.

They would have found the time and discipline, and even wanted to practice, had two things occurred. First, they would have needed to understand the mechanics of good practice. In other words, they would have needed to understand how proper mechanics would make their experience of the learning process efficient and free of stress and impatience. Second, they would have needed to experience a shift in their intended goal. We have a very unhealthy habit of making the *product* — our intended result — the goal, instead of the *process* of reaching that goal. This is evident in many activities in our everyday lives. We become fixated on our intended goal and completely miss out on the joy present in the process of achieving it. We erroneously think that there is a magical point that we will reach and then we will be happy. We look at the *process* of getting there as almost a necessary nuisance we have to go through in order to get to our goal.

Let's look at both of the points mentioned above. It will become apparent that they are interrelated and that one creates the other. First, we will look at the difference between practicing something and just learning it. To begin, let's define what the word *practice* means in its simplest form.

To me, the words *practice* and *learning* are similar but not the same. The word *practice* implies the presence of awareness and will. The word *learning* does not. When we practice something, we are involved in *the deliberate repetition of a process with the intention of reaching a specific goal*. The words *deliberate* and *intention* are key here because they define the difference between actively practicing something and passively learning it. If you grow up in a household where there is constant bickering and inappropriate behavior, you can *learn* that behavior without your knowledge. If that happens, then in order for you to change similar bickering behavior within yourself, you must first become *aware* of the personality tendencies you possess, and practice a different behavior repeatedly and deliberately with the *intention* of changing.

Practice encompasses learning, but not the other way around. Learning does not take content into consideration. Keeping that in mind, we can also say that good practice mechanics require deliberately and intentionally *staying* in the process of doing something and being aware of whether or not we are actually accomplishing that. This also requires that we let go of our attachment to the "product."

The title of this chapter is "Process, Not Product." This simple and yet powerful statement is something I am sure you have heard in one form or another at some time in your life. Sayings such as "Stay on purpose," "Don't be too results-oriented," and "There is no goal in life; life is the goal" are all stating the same truth. What these are all saying is "focus on the *process*, not the product that the process was meant to achieve." It's a paradox. When you focus on the process, the desired product takes care of itself with fluid ease. When you focus on the product, you immediately begin to fight yourself and experience boredom, restlessness, frustration, and impatience with the process. The reason for this is not hard to understand. When you focus your mind on the present moment, on the *process* of what you are doing right now, you are always where you want to be and where you should be. All your energy goes into what you are doing. However, when you focus your mind on where you want to end up, you are never where you are, and you exhaust your energy with unrelated thoughts instead of putting it into what you are doing.

In order to focus on the present, we must give up, at least temporarily, our attachment to our desired goal. If we don't give up our attachment to the goal, we cannot be in the present because we are thinking about something that hasn't occurred yet: the goal. This is the goal shift I spoke of earlier. When you shift your goal from the product you are trying to achieve to the process of achieving it, a wonderful phenomenon occurs: all pressure drops away. This happens because, when your goal is to pay attention to only what you are doing right now, as long as you are doing just that, you are reaching your goal in each and every moment. In one respect, this is a very subtle shift, but in another, it's a tremendous leap in how you approach anything that requires your effort. When you truly shift into putting your attention on what you are doing right now and remain continually aware that you are doing so, you begin to feel calm, refreshed, and in control. Your mind slows down because you are asking it to think only of one thing at a time. The inner chatter drops away. Focusing in this manner is very contrary to how we handle most of our activities during the day. Our minds try to manage a long list of things that we need to get done (in the future) or forgot to do (in the past). We are everywhere but *where* we are, and we are usually doing too many things at once.

This awareness of being where you are and in the present gives you the constant positive reinforcement of reaching your goal over and over again. However, when your mind is only on the finished product, not only do you feel frustrated in every second that you have not met that goal, but you experience anxiety in every "mistake" you make while practicing. You view each mistake as a barrier, something delaying you from realizing your goal and experiencing the joy that reaching that goal is going to give you.

When, instead, your goal is to focus on the process and stay in the present, then there are no mistakes and no judging. You are just learning and doing. You are executing the activity, observing the outcome, and adjusting yourself and your practice energy to produce the desired result. There are no bad emotions, because you are not judging anything.

Using music as an example, let's say you are trying to learn a particular piece of music. If your goal is to play the entire piece of music perfectly, with each note you play you will be making constant judgments about the music and yourself: "I played that part correctly, but I can't seem to get this part right." "Here comes the part I always mess up." "It will never sound the way I want. This is hard work." All these judgments require your energy, and none of that energy is going into learning the music and getting to a point where it is effortless for you to play it. These thoughts are only keeping you from learning the piece of music. We waste so much of our energy by not being aware of how we are directing it.

This doesn't mean that you must lose touch with what you are aiming for. You continue to use the final goal as a rudder to steer your practice session, but not as an indicator of how you are doing. The goal creates a dilemma in any activity you choose, because it is usually the reason you undertake an endeavor in the first place, and it is always out there as a point of comparison against which to measure your progress. You can really see this dilemma in sports such as skating, gymnastics, bowling, and golf, which have "perfect" scores, but in more subtle ways it is also present in any area of life where we aspire to accomplish something. If, while writing this book, I start to feel that I just want to get this chapter done so I can move on to the next, I am doing the same thing and misusing the goal. If you are trying to improve how you deal with a difficult coworker, and one day you slip a little in your effort and then judge yourself for that, you are doing the same thing and misusing the goal. The problem is everywhere, in everything we do. In the particular case just mentioned, you could just stay in the present, observe your interaction with your colleague, use how you want to deal with the situation (your goal) as a rudder, and then readjust yourself so that you are in the process of sailing toward that goal.

You could think of it as throwing tennis balls into a trash can from ten feet away. Imagine that I gave you three tennis balls and told you to throw them one at a time into a trash can ten feet away. The most productive way to perform the task is something like this: You pick up a tennis ball, look at the trash can, and toss the first ball. If the ball hits the floor in front of the can, you observe this and make the decision to adjust the arc of the ball and how hard you will toss the next ball based on this observed information. You continue this process with each toss, allowing present-moment feedback to help you refine the art of tossing a tennis ball into a trash can.

Where we fall down in this activity is when we drop out of this present-minded approach and become attached to the outcome of our attempts. Then we start the emotional judgment cycle: "How could I have missed the first one? I am not very good at this. Now the best I can do is two out of three," and on and on. If we stay in the *process*, this does not occur. We look at the outcome of each attempt with emotional indifference. We accept it as it is, with no judgment involved.

Remember, judgment redirects and wastes our energy. One could argue that we must judge the outcome of each attempt to make a decision about how to proceed, but this is not true. Judgment brings a sense of right or wrong, good or bad with it. What we are doing here is objectively observing and analyzing the outcome of each attempt. This observation serves only to direct our next effort. It is amazing how everything changes when we use this way of thinking to approach any new activity. For one thing, we become patient with ourselves. We are not in a hurry to get to some predetermined point. Our goal is to stay in this process and to direct our energy into whatever activity we are choosing at the present. Every second that we achieve this, we fulfill our goal. This process brings us inner peace and a wonderful sense of mastery and self-confidence. We are mastering ourselves by staying in the process and mastering whatever activity we are working on. This is the essence of proper practice.

Why are we so poor at all of this? How did we learn to process life in such a contrary manner, one that screams that the product is the only concern? This mentality pushes us harder and harder, with no end in sight. By not staying in the process, our minds dash all over the place all day long, the horses running free with no one at the reins. We think too many thoughts at once, most of them the same thoughts we had yesterday and the day before. We are impatient with life, and anxious.

We must accept that, to a certain extent, such thinking is human nature. If you read about any of the great world religions and philosophies, you will find that at their core is the subject of our inability to stay in the present moment. They all speak at great length about how overcoming this is everything in realizing and experiencing true inner peace and attaining real self-empowerment. Hence the millennia-old story of the chariot driver.

In the West, we can blame at least a certain amount of our product orientation on the way our culture operates. This weakness in human nature is repeatedly taught to us and incorporated into our personalities, which makes becoming aware of, let alone overcoming, this crippling perspective all the more difficult.

In sports, we focus on who won. In an art form such as music, a new student asks, "How long will it take me to play like that person over there?" as if every moment up to that point will be drudgery that must be endured. In education, as we will discuss, what we truly learn is at best a footnote, because in the end it is a school's output of high grades that determines its future funding. For most of our culture, focusing on the process is almost frowned upon; it's seen as missing the point.

The idea that the end product is all that really matters starts when we are very young. Even if we do not remember exactly what behaviors we observed in early childhood to instill this idea into our personalities, it is surely there for most of us by the time we get to school age. If any of us are lucky enough to fail to acquire this perspective before that time, you can be sure that our educational systems will work to instill it.

To expand on the point made above, school is the beginning of what I will refer to as hard, fast *markers* that define who we are. These markers are, of course, grades. Grades, when functioning properly, should inform the educational system about how well the present method of teaching is working. However, whether they actually accomplish this is up for discussion. Grades in school have been around for a long time, and people still get everything from As to Fs on their report cards. Standardized Achievement Tests are another form of grading our performance in academic matters. They heavily influence which colleges we get into and whether a particular school will even consider us as potential students. During our school years, our grade accomplishments very much define who we are and what we are worth. They can greatly influence not only how far we will go in life but in what direction we will head. They speak much to us about our sense of self-worth. Someone who scores mostly Cs feels that he is "Average." An F student is a "Failure," and an A student is, of course, "Excellent." During our school years, we begin to develop a bottom-line belief that states, "Results are everything," regardless of how we achieve them. Why else would people cheat?

I am not here to promote a New Age scoring system that makes us all feel that we are head-of-the-class material. That would be beyond both the context of this book and my ability. What is within the context of this book is how the grading system affects our attitudes toward making the *product* the priority, rather than the *process*.

All through my school years I found math to be a most difficult subject. Even at a very early age, certain aspects of math just didn't make sense to me. The teacher would go over something new on the board, and I would listen intently and try to follow, but to no avail. I would start on the new assignment with a resolve to overcome my lack of understanding with hard work, but it never seemed to help. I was very much a creative-minded child, not an analytical one in the mathematical sense. My grades always reflected this, and my report cards consistently showed I was somewhat of a B student, with an A sprinkled in here and there, except in math. In subjects that were more right-brained, such as creative writing, I was usually the first one done with assignments. In math, I was working after the bell had rung and most of the other students had left. Some of my trouble was probably due to poor instruction. I say this because there were one or two math teachers who presented the material to me in a way that was very clear, and I could manage at least a B or C grade in those classes, but they were the exception to the rule.

What I learned about myself through the experience of school and grades illustrates how the product becomes the priority instead of the process. Most of us heard phrases during our school years that were actually rooted in the correct mindset of "process, not product." I am speaking of encouraging words such as "just try your hardest; that's what is important" and "do your best; that's all anyone can ask." These phrases were very good advice, but somehow most of us knew they were empty, bogus statements. In regard to math, I can honestly say I did try my hardest, but that never consoled me when I got my report card. I would immediately skip through the Cs, Bs, and As that were scattered through the columns and go right to "Math Comprehension," where the D (most likely a gift for trying hard) sat as big as life. I was very fortunate to have parents who were unimpressed with academic achievements. They were always encouraging, despite the low grades I received. Still, in those elementary school days and all the way through college, I carried an inner perception that those grades were who I was and a measure of my self-worth, at least as far as math went. I learned to dread math of any kind, and I felt inadequate in my ability to overcome that feeling.

I was not alone in this perspective, by any stretch of the imagination. Some people, perhaps those whose parents were very invested in academic achievement, had an even stronger commitment to the power of the grade. An example of this was when I took a music theory course at a local college when I was twenty-five years old and living on my own. I owned a business that supported me, and the decision to take the course was strictly my own. Because I was self-employed, I had the luxury of not having to take a night class. I could get right into the day class with the fresh-out-of-high-school kids.

One of the assignments in this class was to work on a computer whose program tested us on all the material that was covered in class. It graded us on each area of the work, and it did not allow us to advance to the next lesson until we had passed the one we were presently on. The Big Brother nature of the whole system made things worse. We worked in a lab full of computers, as you would expect, but they were all centrally networked. The professor could log into our lessons any time he wanted to and see exactly where we were in the curriculum. This was before the days of the Internet and household networking, so the concept seemed very futuristic and somewhat daunting. As if all this were not enough, we had a time element to contend with. We were allowed only so much time to give each answer. What was particularly bad about this was that our class was unknowingly a test group. We were being timed, but a sister class covering the same lesson plan was not. We however did not know that we were the only ones with a time constraint on our answers.

I won't go into how I uncovered this secret, but what

I learned was that someone in the college wanted to see if the students would learn the same material faster if put under a time constraint. This was an interesting idea, except that, since we were the first attempt at this procedure, the faculty didn't really know what a reasonable amount of time would be to give a student to calculate the answers to the computer's questions. They grossly underestimated, and no one was able to answer the questions in the time allotted. A correct answer that took too long to type in was considered wrong by the computer, and hence a failure. Our frustration was compounded by the fact that the computer-lab work counted as 33 percent of our final grade in the class.

On the first day of class, we received a schedule sheet describing our expected progress on the computer on each day. Virtually no one could come even close to meeting this schedule, and the farther behind students got, the more stressed they felt. One day the professor made the mistake of stating rather casually that people were not keeping up with their computer work and reminding us to not forget the impact of this on our grade. The unexpected reaction he received was frighteningly reminiscent of the old westerns in which an angry mob hunted for a good rope and a tree to go with it.

At this point, the faculty did not realize that they had put students in a no-win situation. They assumed that the time allotment was sufficient and fair and that the reason for the students' difficulties was that they were not putting in enough time. Students, in reality, were putting in way too much time, and were even neglecting other classes in an effort to catch up in this class. Some of them were visibly distraught.

Yet I was immune to all this angst because I was an adult student. I had paid for my class and I really didn't care about the grade I received. I was interested only in information that would be helpful in my musical composing efforts. I didn't have to mail a copy of my grade home to my parents, because I was on my own. Because I was older than the rest of the students, I also had the perspective that this class wasn't going to make or break my life. I had failed tests before and I was still here. I felt almost like a wizened parent watching children react to something that, to them, was so important and yet at some point down the road would seem so insignificant.

The point of this story was how the other students resolved the problem. In short, they cheated. They very blatantly cheated. Anyone could go into the computer lab at any time. It was open twenty-four hours a day, seven days a week, and the professor was never around. Once the students found out what the questions would be, they would write down all the answers on a memo pad and walk into the lab, setting the pad on their laps. Before the computer finished asking the question, they were typing in the answer. They caught up on all their work, received perfect scores, and felt very justified in their actions. Unfortunately, they learned little to nothing about music theory.

When I was working on an assignment at a computer and talking to them, I would hear the same thing over and over again: "This class and this computer are not going to ruin my grade." The *grade* was everything; the knowledge was nothing. They finished the course with a piece of paper that had an A on it that meant nothing. They had learned almost nothing during the three months (the process), but they felt that they had won because of the grade they had received (the product). But what did they really gain that was of any lasting value?

On the other hand, what choice did they have? Our culture is a bottom-line, results-oriented society. Corporations will hire a 4.0 before a 2.0 every time because they feel the 4.0 has more to offer. To them, the 4.0 is who you are and what your future potential is. With regard to this particular situation, if a student had instead said, "Forget the grade," and expended all her energy on just learning as much of the material as possible, she would have had no valid way to represent what she had accomplished. Our culture does not recognize the value of being process-oriented, even though we see so much evidence for it in the work produced by countries that do.

Back in the midseventies, there was a real upheaval going on in the business world of manufacturing. Everyone wanted Japanese automobiles because they were noticeably higher in quality than American ones. American auto manufacturers were scrambling to understand why this was so and how to fix it. But this wasn't a situation limited to the auto industry. Japanese pianos were becoming popular in this country. Some of them had names people had never heard before and couldn't even pronounce properly, but they could see the quality difference in them regardless. The Japanese were very process-oriented in their lives and work. We had trouble competing with them because we couldn't duplicate their work environment or their mindset, which was so different from ours.

A major piano retailer for whom I performed service related a story to me that really illustrated the primary differences between the two cultures. He had gone to Japan and taken a tour of a plant that manufactured a piano he sold in his store. While walking down the assembly line, he observed a worker whose job was to prepare the piano plate (the big gold harp assembly that holds all the strings) after it had come out of the casting. These plates are made from cast iron, and when they come out of the mold, they are pretty rough looking. The plate must undergo grinding and polishing before it can be painted. The finished Japanese plates are absolutely flawless and beautiful. As the worker prepared a plate, my retailer friend asked him how many plates he finished in a day. The Japanese worker, confused, looked at him and answered, "As many as I can make perfect."

The retailer asked, "But don't you have a supervisor to report to?"

"What is a supervisor?" asked the worker.

"Someone to make sure you do your job correctly," answered the retailer.

"Why would I need someone to make sure I do my job correctly?" answered the Japanese worker. "That's my job."

We can't begin to conceive of a mindset like this. If it took all day to make one perfect plate, he had done his job correctly and fulfilled the company's expectations of his position. The job required him to focus his mind in the present and keep it there. By practicing this right thinking, he produced the best work and maintained a fresh, uncluttered mind. One perfect plate was more important than twenty acceptable ones.

The Japanese use of the goal (in this case, a perfect plate) as their rudder and their knowledge that this patient approach would yield a much stronger result in the long run enabled them to outcompete American factories. They completely upset the automotive and music industries, not to mention the electronics industry.

We, on the other hand, can't wait that long for anything. We want the product, and we want it now. Skip the process altogether and get to the product. We are obsessed with getting everything immediately. Credit card debt soars and ruins many people in this country because it feeds on this mindset of "Get it now and pay for it later." Credit cards work on the premise of product *before* process, instead of process first. This mentality leads only to a general sense of nonfulfillment and emptiness. We have all experienced a situation where we wanted something very much but didn't have the money for it, so we charged it.

The fulfillment from attaining the object is usually gone long before the first bill arrives.

We have phrases that describe our addiction to this mindset. "Instant gratification" is one of them. It would be more accurately stated as "Instant gratification, short-term satisfaction" because anything we acquire in this way has no real, lasting value to us. You can recall everything you worked hard and patiently for in your life, but how many things that you have attained with little or no effort can you remember? When we focus our energy on the process of attaining something, whether it be an object or a skill, and through patience and discipline we achieve it, we experience a joy that is just not present when something comes too quickly or easily. In fact, when we reminisce about something we tried to acquire, the process is what comes to mind, not the object itself. We remember our mastery of our undisciplined nature, the patience and perseverance that we developed, and the joy and satisfaction we experienced then. What we remember is timeless, because we experience it all over again.

I have no attachment to my first car, which I worked and saved for all summer twenty-five years ago, but I can remember every detail of the work I performed to earn the money. I worked three jobs simultaneously. When my friends were off to the beach or lounging around, I stuck with it, and by the end of the summer I was the only one driving my own car. Once, when I was getting a little impatient to buy a car before I really had enough money, my father said something very profound to me. He said, "You are going to find out that buying the car is much less satisfying than working for it." He was right, and I never forgot those words. Once I bought the car, it was somewhat of a letdown compared with the anticipation of owning it that I had experienced while I was working toward the purchase.

The "get it now" perspective is not just an individual one. Our whole culture participates in it at many levels and in many ways. Corporations are more interested in short-term profits than the long-term health of their organizations and employees. Strangely, if you ask most people, they will agree that this attitude reigns in our society, but we seem to be on a runaway train. We need to pull the brake, and doing that must start within ourselves. Once we experience the shift to a present moment, "process, not product" perspective, we know that it is right. We calm down. Our priorities adjust themselves, and we feel peaceful and fulfilled by what we have and where we are. That age-old saying "There is no destination in life; life is the destination" has real meaning.

So let's go back to my golfing classmates. What could have changed their experience and motivated them to participate in their goal of improving their golf games? If they had made the shift into a "process, not product" mode, their mechanics would have followed. They would have stayed in the present and worked on their swings with deliberation and an awareness of their intention. Their feelings toward working at their golf swings would have changed, and their false sense that "Until I get good at this, I am not going to enjoy the game or feel like practicing" would have vanished. The shift to the "process, not product" mindset would have discarded such feelings, and instead of procrastinating their practice sessions, they would have looked forward to them.

In summary, creating the practicing mind comes down to a few simple rules:

- Keep yourself process-oriented.
- Stay in the present.
- Make the process the goal and use the overall goal as a rudder to steer your efforts.
- Be deliberate, have an intention about what you want to accomplish, and remain aware of that intention.

Doing these things will eliminate the judgments and emotions that come from a product-oriented, results-driven mind.

When you remain aware of your intention to stay focused on the present, it's easy to notice when you fall out of this perspective. At such times you immediately begin to judge what and how well you are doing, and you experience impatience and boredom. When you catch yourself in these moments, just gently remind yourself that you have fallen out of the present, and feel good about the fact that you are now aware enough to recognize it. You have begun to develop the Observer within you, who will prove so important in your self-guidance.

Understand that this exercise, while not the easiest one you have ever undertaken, is probably the most important. As I said earlier, all the major philosophies and religions speak at great length about the value of focusing on the present in order to gain personal empowerment and inner happiness. If you do begin to succumb to discouragement, remember the words at the start of this chapter: The problem with patience and discipline is that developing each of them requires both of them.

*As we attempt to understand ourselves
and our struggles with life's endeavors,
we may find peace in the observation
of a flower. Ask yourself:
At what point in a flower's life,
from seed to full bloom,
does it reach perfection?*

CHAPTER 3

It's How You Look at It

Most of the anxiety we experience in life comes from our feeling that there is an end point of perfection in everything that we involve ourselves with. Whatever or wherever that perfection may be, we are not. We continually examine, consciously or unconsciously, everything in our lives, compare it to what we feel is ideal, and then judge where we are in relation to that ideal. Having a bigger home, earning more income, and buying a certain kind of car are all normal parts of this routine.

There's a very compelling scene in a famous movie (and novel) *The Natural* about a baseball player who is injured just as he begins to appear on the professional scene. He possesses almost mystical powers when it comes to playing baseball, and he is poised to become the most famous player who ever lived. But his injury happens during an embarrassing situation, so he disappears from view for many years. Eventually he comes back and, although he is now middle-aged, his incredible talents enable him to play on a pro team. He becomes a hero in short order, but his injury, which never fully healed, resurfaces and he ends up in the hospital.

It is here that I think a profound line is spoken. Reminiscing dejectedly with his childhood sweetheart about what might have been, he says, "I coulda been better. I coulda broke every record in the book." Her response is so simple and yet so shattering: "And then?" That two-word line carries such power. A runner breaks the four-minute mile, and then? A soloist plays her most difficult piece of music in concert without a mistake for the first time, and then? A golfer finally breaks 90, an entrepreneur makes his first million, and then? All these personal images of perfection dissolve quickly into a newer image: a faster time, a more difficult piece, a lower score, more money.

The problem with these ideal images is that they may not be realistic or even attainable, and in general they have nothing to do with true happiness. In fact, these images are handed to us by marketing and the media. We watch all these perfect-looking people on TV and in the movies living their perfect lives. In TV advertisements, this illusion is presented even more strongly: "Buy this and your life will be great," or, worse yet, "Without this, your life is incomplete." Automobile commercials are particularly amusing in their overemphasis on these messages. They present ownership of their particular car as some sort of euphoric experience. In reality, we all know that cars are terrible investments that depreciate faster than anything else, and that when we purchase a new one, we spend most of our mental energy worrying that it will be stolen or damaged in the local mall parking lot. Plus, although in the commercial the driver cruised some deserted backroad full of farms, switchbacks, and autumn scenery, we sit in a traffic jam on the expressway. Still, ads continue to show us all the products we need to buy to complete our lives' yearnings, from cars to clothes to beverages.

You can learn a lot about yourself by watching the commercials that come on during your favorite programming. You can be sure the advertiser has spent a lot of money finding out which personality profile watches a particular type of program before deciding which shows to sponsor. Advertisers also take it one step further by stipulating to networks which types of programming will attract an audience who will be receptive to their ads.

How we arrive at these ideal images of perfection, though, is not as important as becoming aware of how they distort our perspective of where we are on the road to happiness. If these images are used for inspiration, they can be very beneficial; but if they are used as a measuring device, they can become our downfall. For example, you could go out to a concert one evening and hear the performance of a world-class piano soloist. The next day, so moved by the performance the night before, you could decide to take up the piano. If you buy a CD of the soloist playing the performance you heard the previous night and use it to motivate yourself to practice, it could be a very good thing. If, however, you begin to analyze your progress based on how you play in relation to the soloist's performance (something that is usually done unconsciously), you are headed for discontentment and may even become so frustrated that you give up on your efforts.

If you don't believe that you do this, look more closely at yourself. We all do. That is why advertising works so well. It preys upon our sense that "all is not right until I get to such and such a point." Whether that point is owning a particular item or reaching a particular status is not important. What is necessary in overcoming this nature is to become aware that we have the potential to perceive life in this manner and to know that our culture reinforces our tendencies toward it. We look in the mirror and judge our looks based on present fashion trends and whether we fit them. Go out on a golf course and you will see somebody slamming a club into the ground because he missed a particular shot that might have been way beyond his ability. His ideal and point of reference, however, is a pro he watched on TV who hits five hundred balls a day with a swing coach observing, and who plays five days a week. This is what I mean by unrealistic and perhaps unattainable ideal images. The amateur in question probably plays once a week, has had a few lessons, and hits maybe a hundred balls a week. Yet his or her standard is the epitome of the sport.

We make a major detour on the road to happiness when we adopt an image of perfection in anything. This is because an image or ideal is frozen and stagnant, and limited by nature. An ideal implies that it is as good as a particular circumstance or thing can get. True perfection, in contrast, is limitless, unbounded, and always expanding. We can gain a much more productive and satisfying perspective by studying the life of a flower.

Reread the opening phrase for this chapter: As we attempt to understand ourselves and our struggles with life's endeavors, we may find peace in the observation of a flower. Ask yourself: At what point in a flower's life, from seed to full bloom, does it reach perfection?

Let's see what nature teaches us every day as we walk past the flowers in our garden. At what point is a flower perfect? Is it perfect when it is nothing more than a seed in your hand waiting to be planted? All that it will ever be is there in that moment. Is it perfect when it first starts to germinate unseen under several inches of soil? This is when it displays the first signs of the miracle we call creation. How about when it pokes its head through the surface and sees the face of the sun for the first time? All its energies have gone into reaching for this source of life; until this point, it has had nothing more than an inner voice telling it which way to grow. What about when it begins to flower? This is when its individual properties start to be seen. The shape of the leaves, the number of blooms: all are unique to this one flower, even among the other flowers of the same species. Or is it the stage of full bloom, the crescendo of all the energy and effort the flower expended to reach this point in its life? Let's not forget its humble and quiet ending, when it returns to the soil from where it came. At what point is the flower perfect?

I hope you already know the answer: It is *always* perfect. It is perfect at being wherever it is and at whatever stage of growth it is in at that moment. It is perfect at being a seed, when it is placed into the ground. At that moment in time, it is exactly what it is supposed to be: a seed. Just because it does not have brightly colored blooms doesn't mean it is not a good flower seed. When it first sprouts through the ground, it is not imperfect because it displays only the color green. At each stage of growth, from seed to full bloom and beyond, it is perfect at being a flower at that particular stage of a flower's life. A flower must start as a seed, and it will not budge one millimeter toward its potential grandeur of full bloom without the nourishment of water, soil, sun, and also *time*. It takes time for all these elements to work together to produce the flower.

Do you think that a flower seed sits in the ground and says, "This is going to take forever. I have to push all this dirt out of my way just to get to the surface and see the sun. Every time it rains or somebody waters me, I'm soaking wet and surrounded by mud. When do I get to bloom? That's when I'll be happy; that's when everybody will be impressed with me. I hope I'm an orchid and not some wildflower nobody notices. Orchids have it all...no, wait; I want to be an oak tree. They are bigger than anybody else in the forest and live longer, too"?

As silly as the flower's monologue might sound, it is exactly what we do, and we do it, as they say, every day and in every way. We consciously or unconsciously pick a point of reference in whatever we do and decide that nothing will be right until we get to that point. If you step back and observe your internal dialogue from time to time during the day, you will be amazed at how hard you work against yourself with this type of thinking.

When we are driving somewhere, we can't wait to get *there*. Wherever *there* is, I doubt very much it often matters whether we arrive fifteen minutes later than we'd expected. Yet when I am driving on the highway, all around me people are pushing the speed limit to the maximum and probably never notice most of what they drive past. When I look in my rearview mirror, I see someone who is irritated with the world for getting in his way and exhausted by the stress and strain that impatience brings to his body and mind when he lives in this state. If you step back routinely during your day and observe where your attention is, you will be amazed at how few times it is where you are and on what you are doing.

When you develop a present-minded approach to every activity you are involved in and, like the flower, realize that at whatever level you are performing, you are perfect at that point in time, you experience a tremendous relief from the fictitious, self-imposed pressures and expectations that only slow your progress. At any point in the day when you notice you are feeling bored, impatient, rushed, or disappointed with your performance level, realize that you have left the present moment in your activity. Look at where your mind and energy are focused.

You will find that you have strayed into either the future or the past. You might be subconsciously focused on the result or product you are trying to achieve. Such feelings often arise in activities that produce a tangible product, which could be anything from painting the house to losing weight. I class this as a distraction into the future because the product that you want to reach is pulling you out of the present and into the future. You want to get to "full bloom" and skip the rest of it.

Sometimes, though, it is not a tangible thing that pulls us away from the present, but a circumstance. Imagine this: You are standing in your kitchen preparing dinner and your child or spouse is telling you about his day. Are you looking into his eyes when he is talking to you? Are you fully listening to what he is sharing with you in this present moment, or are you half listening while you anticipate going someplace after dinner or thinking of something you said to someone at work that day that you regret?

Stop yourself during the day as much as you can and ask yourself, "Am I practicing flower-like qualities and staying in the present with my thoughts and energies?" Nature knows what works because it does not have an ego to deal with. It is our ego that makes us create false ideas of what perfect is and whether we have reached it. As I said earlier, true perfection is not finite. It is not a specific number, as in how much you weigh or how much you make. It is not a specific skill level that can be reached regardless of how long and how hard you pursue an activity. Any high-level performers in any sport or art form will tell you this: Their idea of perfection is always moving away from them; it is always based on their present experience and perspective. When we learn this truth, we really get on the path toward true, authentic happiness. We realize that, like the flower, we are just fine or, rather, that we are perfect when we are where we are and absorbed in what we are doing right at that moment. With this perspective, our impatience to reach some false goal that will not make us any happier than we are right now fades away.

We can learn so much from nature by simply observing how it works through a flower. The flower knows it is part of nature; we have forgotten that. Remember, the reason we bother ourselves with a lifelong effort to gain a practicing mind is not to be able to say, "I have mastered the technique of present-moment awareness." This is an ego-based statement. We work at it for one reason: it brings us the inner peace and happiness that we cannot attain through the acquisition of any material object or cultural status. What we achieve is timeless, always with us, and perhaps the only thing that we can really call our own. The stamina needed to pursue a present-moment attitude daily comes naturally when we realize that our current attitudes leave us longing for something we can't seem to put our finger on. Despite all our achievements and acquisitions in life, we still feel a longing to fill the emptiness inside. We may not have even consciously admitted our emptiness to ourselves, but our need for answers is still there. If it were not, we wouldn't be reading material such as this book.

Present-minded awareness can be and is a natural state when the circumstances are right. In fact, we all have experienced this state of mind many times in our lives. The problem in identifying at what times we are functioning in this state is a paradox. When we are totally focused on the present moment and in the process of what we are doing, we are completely absorbed in the activity. As soon as we become aware of how well we are concentrating on something, we are no longer concentrating on it. We are now concentrating on the fact that we *were* concentrating on the activity. When we are practicing correctly, we are not aware we are practicing correctly. We are only aware and absorbed in the process of what we are doing in that moment.

In Zen, this state is referred to as "beginner's mind." When you are a beginner in any activity, accomplishing it takes all your concentration, and your mind is empty of chatter. As you become more adept at the activity, concentrating solely on performing it actually becomes harder. Remember when you first started learning to drive a car? You were totally absorbed in the process of learning to drive the car. You had a beginner's mind. Now when you drive, you have lost that beginner's mind. You are listening to the radio, which you would have considered a distraction in the beginning. You are having a conversation with someone in the car or thinking of something you have to do later that day. Your mind is someplace other than where you are, and on something other than what you are doing. The next time you get into the car, try to think of nothing other than driving the car. Try to keep your awareness on where other drivers are and what they are doing, how the scenery looks, and how your hands are placed on the wheel. If you are alone, try to stop any internal dialogue, and turn off the radio. It will feel maddening. You will find it impossible to give up your awareness that you are trying to *not* think of anything but driving the car. What was so simple and natural when you had no driving skills at all will be seemingly impossible to repeat now that you are fully competent. The point of this exercise is not to make us feel that we can't accomplish the desired mindset through effort, but to help us understand how we behave and feel when we are *in* it.

This is also the true purpose of the martial arts. Hollywood has made the martial arts seem a form of acrobatics performed by superhumans whose goal is to take on any number of opponents and easily defeat them, but this is far removed from the original nature of the martial arts. The different forms of martial arts serve to teach the participants how to function in the present moment and to force them into this state of mind through a desire for self-preservation. The student diligently works at all the moves of the particular form he or she is studying. These moves are *deliberately* performed over and over again with *intention* and *awareness*, to a point of repletion. They become totally reflexive and intuitive.

When two students spar in a ring, they are completely

focused on the present moment. They are aware of where they are in relationship to their opponent and what their opponent is doing. They observe each second as it comes at them and react instinctively to the motion of the opponent. When your mind wanders in a situation like this, you're quickly aware of it (you get hurt). There is no time to think of anything but the process of both offense and defense. In each second, you must be ready to both defend yourself or get out of the way of your opponent's advance and make your own strike when the opportunity presents itself. These sparring matches give the participants the opportunity to experience the instinctive, total present-moment awareness that occurs during life-threatening situations without their actually being in any lethal danger.

If you imagine yourself in a situation such as this, you will see that, during a present-moment experience, you cannot be aware of anything other than the experience itself. This is why we cannot observe ourselves when we are practicing a process-oriented mentality. What we *can* do is use the moments of questioning whether we are focusing on the process to remind us that we are not.

Even though we cannot directly observe ourselves when we are functioning in a process-oriented, present-minded state, we can observe this state quite easily in others. One of the best examples of this is to watch someone play a computer video game. You will see perfect practice in action. Video games offer a natural environment for pulling us into a state of focused present-moment awareness.

In a video game, the score is essentially the end result or product that the player is working for, but the game itself is where the fun is. The process of playing the game takes all your attention. If you take more than a second to glance at the score, it can make or break your attempt to beat the computer at the game. If you watch people playing a computer game, you will observe how totally focused they are on what they are doing in that moment. Even though the best score possible is the ultimate goal, the participants are only superficially aware of it. The process of playing the game requires all their attention. If you talk to people playing a computer game, they may not even answer you because they are so absorbed in the process of the game. Watching a movie can have the same effect on us if we find it particularly interesting. We say it "captivates" us because it captures our attention.

Most of us find that we are very good at practicing properly during recreational activities. We perform these activities with all our attention in the present and on what we are doing. What is the difference, then, between work activities and recreational activities? Why do we find it so much easier to focus on something we consider play than on something we consider work? If we can find answers to these questions, they could help us advance our efforts toward operating in a present-minded state all the time.

I have found that the only difference between the two sorts of activities is that we prejudge them. We make a conscious decision that if we enjoy an activity, it is not work. So we must temporarily suspend our definition of *work* as referring to our daily vocation. *Work*, in this discussion, refers to any activity we don't feel like doing, and though it could certainly include our job duties, or at least parts of them, it could also include any activity that we think is "undesirable."

We know that this prejudgment of whether an activity is work or play is not universal, because one person's hobby is another person's drudgery. Some people love to garden; others don't even want to cut the grass. I watched a program one evening called *The Joy of Snakes*. To me, that's a self-contradictory title, but to the show's host, it made perfect sense.

The knowledge that we prejudge our activities and then place them into one of the two categories is very powerful. It demonstrates to us that nothing is really work or play. We make an activity into work or play by our judgments. The next time you find yourself doing something that you really don't feel like doing, stop for a moment and ask yourself why. What is it about the activity that makes you feel that way? You will find that many times you really can't put your finger on why you don't want to do something. You will end up saying, "I just don't feel like doing this right now." This implies that what you feel like doing is something else that you have defined as "not work." You are not in the present but instead are in the future, anticipating another activity.

But why, during a subconscious judgment process, do we define one activity as work and another as "not work"? I feel that a large part of what makes us define something as work is that the activity requires a lot of decision making, which can be very stressful and fatiguing. This is especially true when the decisions that you are making are very subtle and you are not even aware that you are making them.

Once, when I was preparing a concert piano for an orchestra and soloist, I found myself going through the experience of "I just don't feel like doing this." As I tried to put my finger on exactly why I felt this way, I realized it was due to the hundreds of decisions I was having to make during the tuning process and the responsibility that went along with them. When the soloist came out to perform that evening, all his years of practicing and preparation would go out the window if I hadn't set up this instrument correctly. My stress was generated by my concern about making the wrong decision, for which I would be held accountable. When I started to examine why I was lacking in confidence about something in which I had proven my expertise over and over again, I realized it was because I wasn't working in the present moment. I knew that I wasn't really giving my full attention to what I was doing. I was thinking about something I was going to do later in the day that I had defined as "not work." I subconsciously knew that I wasn't putting all my energy into the process of preparing the piano because, being so adept at it, I had lost that beginner's mind I mentioned earlier. I had tuned a whole section of the instrument, yet I couldn't remember doing it because I had been in the future, daydreaming.

Here is another, similar workplace example of this

that may sound familiar. One day, while a close friend and I discussed these ideas, she related a story about a situation in her office. Here is what she shared with me. A payroll processor who had a looming deadline to process hundreds of payrolls plugged away at completing her task. Running under the surface in her mind was palpable anxiety about what she might face if she did not complete her task on time and meet her deadline. She might have needed to call a manager to ask for an exception to push through payroll past her deadline. This might not have been the first time she'd had to do this, so another layer of anxiety was added. If she did not make payroll on time, paychecks might have been delayed, followed by email and phone complaints that she would need to deal with on top of her already overburdened workload. A reprimand could have been likely, which possibly would have impacted her annual review. And on and on it went.

All this thought energy drained her, both on the job and when she was at home in the evening. It also constantly tugged her out of the present moment and into the future as she unconsciously considered all these possible stressful scenarios. Under a different circumstance, the act of doing payroll could have had a totally different feeling to it, and for some people, the task might not even have been something they defined as work because the experience that accompanied it didn't have all these background "what-if's" clamoring away.

In this situation, even when she was removed from her

"place of work," she couldn't relax. She was not present mentally with her family and might even have struggled to be present with something she usually defined as "not work." What was worse was that none of the vast amounts of energy she expended in running through these possible scenarios went into the process of completing payroll on time and thus removing this task from her workload. Yet she was most likely unaware that any of this was happening. She was merely thinking, "This is work, and I don't feel like doing it."

One evening, I happened upon an interview with a well-known actor on TV. I watch very little TV because I feel that most of it offers no return for the time you invest in it. But this particular interview caught my ear because I heard the actor talking about how he had gotten into meditating later in his life. The point of his interview, in the context of this book, is that he said he had become very present moment–oriented. He found it increasingly difficult to plan future events because he was so wrapped up in what he was doing *right now*, in *this* moment. He had learned he could completely enjoy anything he was doing, provided he kept his mind in the present and just focused on the process of what he was doing at that moment. The difference this made in his life and how he felt was very profound to him.

Try this the next time you are faced with doing something you define as unenjoyable or as work. It doesn't matter if it is mowing the lawn or cleaning up the dinner dishes. If the activity will take a long time, tell yourself you will work on staying present-moment and process-oriented for just the first half hour. After that, you can hate it as much as usual, but in that first half hour you absolutely will not think of anything but what you are doing. You will not go into the past and think of all the judgments you have made that define this activity as work. You will not go into the future, anticipating when it will be completed, allowing you to participate in an activity that you have defined as "not work." You will just do whatever you are doing right *now* for half an hour. Don't *try* to enjoy it, either, because in that effort you are bringing emotions and struggle into your effort. If you are going to mow the lawn, then accept that all you need to do is cut the grass. You will notice the feeling of the mower as you push it, and how it changes resistance with the undulations of your front yard. You will pay attention and cut as wide a path as possible, not sloppily overlapping the last pass you made as you gawked at the neighbor across the street washing his car. You will smell the cut grass and notice how the grass glows green in the sunlight. Just do this for one half hour of the activity. You will be amazed. Once you experience how an activity as mundane as mowing the grass can be transformed, you will have the motivation to press on, because the potential effect this could have on your life and how you perceive it will become apparent to you.

I am not going to suggest to you that thinking this way is the easiest thing you will ever do, although, as we discussed earlier, you've already done it many times, naturally and effortlessly, when you were learning something for the first time. At those times, though, you were not willfully doing it, and therein lies the difference. When choosing which activity to begin applying this technique to, it is best to begin with something in which you have no strong emotions invested. If you suspect that you owe $5,000 in taxes, choosing taxes as your first activity is probably not a good idea — the emotional content would make the task much harder. However, as you become better at present-minded thinking, you will realize its value when you're approaching emotionally laden activities and negating their power over you. The practicing mind puts you in control of even the most difficult situations and allows you to work with less effort and negative emotion at any activity. This produces inner peace, and you accomplish more with less effort.

In the next chapter, we will discuss techniques for developing the practicing mind as easily as possible.

Habits are learned.
Choose them wisely.

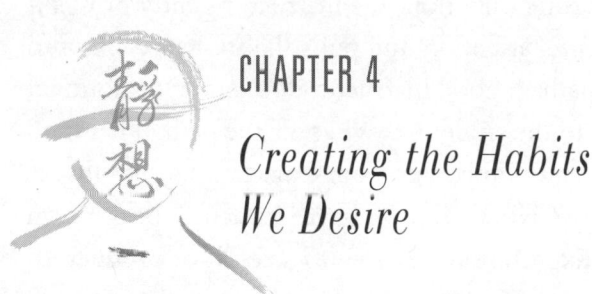

CHAPTER 4

Creating the Habits We Desire

By now, you should notice — or, shall we say, you should be *aware* of — several themes running through this book. One of these themes is awareness itself. You cannot change what you are unaware of. This truth is nowhere more important than in the world of self-improvement. We need to be more aware of what we are doing, what we are thinking, and what we are intending to accomplish in order to gain control of what we experience in life.

But in fact, for most of us, this is a problem because we are so disconnected from our thoughts. We just *have* them. The horses are running, and we don't have the reins. We need to become an observer of our thoughts and actions, like an instructor watching a student performing a task. The instructor is not judgmental or emotional. The instructor knows just what he or she wants the student to produce. The teacher observes the student's actions, and when the student does something that is moving in the wrong direction, the instructor gently brings it to the student's attention and pulls the student back onto the proper path. A good instructor does not get emotional in response to the student moving off the path. That kind of negative emotion comes from expectations, and that is not the perspective we want to have if we are to be our own instructor. Expectations are tied to a result or product, to the thought that "things should be *this* way right now, and until then I won't be happy." When you experience these kinds of emotions, they are indicators that you've fallen out of the process, or out of the present moment.

As when we were throwing tennis balls into a trash can, we should observe what happens, process the information without emotion, and then move on. This is how we should deal with ourselves as we work at learning something new, or when we're changing something about ourselves that we don't like. This includes working on something more abstract, too, such as becoming more *aware* or conscious of what we are thinking, becoming more of an observer of ourselves.

This disconnection from our thoughts and actions is a way of thinking that we have learned during our lives, and one that takes away all our real power. We must unlearn this approach to life. What we are really talking about here is a habit. Everything we do is a habit, in one form or another. How we think, how we talk, how we react to criticism, which type of snack we instinctively reach for:

all are habits. Even when faced with a circumstance for the first time, we respond to it from habit. Whether we observe our thoughts or they just happen in our minds is determined by habits we have learned. We may consider some habits good, others not so good, but all habits can be replaced at will, if you understand how they are formed.

Habits and practice are very interrelated. What we practice will become a habit. This is a very important point because it underscores the value of being in control of our practicing minds. Our minds are going to practice certain behaviors whether or not we are aware of them, and whatever we practice is going to become habit. Knowing this can work in our favor. If we understand how we form habits, and if we become aware of which habits we are forming, we can begin to free ourselves by intentionally creating the habits we want instead of becoming victims of the habits we unknowingly allow to become a part of our behavior. We can gain control of who we are and what we become in life. But what are the mechanics that create a habit? Knowing this would be quite valuable. Fortunately for us, we don't have to figure this out, because others have already done it for us.

The formation of habits has been studied extensively by behavioral scientists and sports psychologists alike. Understanding how desirable habits are created and undesirable habits are replaced is invaluable, particularly in repetitive-motion sports such as golf or diving. In fact, you often see golfers practicing certain parts of their swings over and over again, or divers standing poolside, going through the motions of complex dives they are about to execute. They are practicing and habitualizing their particular moves. What does that mean? To me, when we say that something is a habit, it means that it is the natural way we do something. We do it intuitively, without having to think about it. The martial arts student practices the moves over and over again, habitualizing responses until they become effortless, intuitive, and lightning fast. There is no intellectual process that has to occur in a time of crisis where the brain is saying, "My opponent is doing this, so I must do that." The responses just happen because they are a natural part of the student's behavior. That is what we are after. We want something like being more aware of our thoughts to be just a natural behavior, not something that requires a lot of struggle.

Getting to this point is not complicated. It does take some effort, but the effort is minimal once we understand the process. What is required is that you are aware of what you want to achieve, that you know the motions you must intentionally repeat to accomplish the goal, and that you execute your actions without emotions or judgments; just stay on course. You should do this in the comfort of knowing that intentionally repeating something over a short course of time will create a new habit or replace an old one.

Sports psychologists have gotten very consistent results when studying habit formation. One study states that repeating a particular motion sixty times a day over twenty-one days will form a new habit that will become ingrained in your mind. The sixty repetitions needn't be done all at once but can be broken up into, say, six sets of ten or two sets of thirty during the day. In sports, this type of method can be used to change a certain aspect of a golf swing, or to naturalize any other aspect of a sports motion.

I shoot target archery. The way in which you draw the bow to full tension, and when and how you breathe, is part of good form. Practicing the proper motions many times a day over many days creates a habit of motion that *feels* right and natural and is done without conscious thought. However, you can just as easily haphazardly draw the bow and huff and puff, and that will also become a learned habit. That is why you must be aware that you are forming a habit, know what you want to accomplish, and apply yourself with intentional effort.

Replacing undesirable habits works in the same way. I am sure you have experienced trying to change something that you have done in a certain way for a long time. Initially, the new way feels very strange and awkward because you are moving against the old habit. But in a short period of time, through deliberate repetition, the new way feels normal, and moving back to the old way would feel strange. Once I learned this, the knowledge took much of the stress out of learning something new. It became much easier to stay in the process of doing something new because I wasn't experiencing all the anticipation that results from not having any idea of how long it would take to learn something new. I would just relax and repeat the exercise and stay in the process, knowing that the learning was occurring. Yes, I was applying effort, but there was no sense of struggle. I have used this process extensively while honing my golf skills and learning new passages of music, but also in more personality-related changes.

When I identified something in my behavior that I felt was holding me back or producing undesirable results, I would realize that I had already fulfilled the awareness part of the equation. I would then objectively decide where I wanted to end up and which motions would get me there. Next, I worked through those motions without emotion, knowing that many intentional repetitions over a short period of time would create the behavior I was after. There was no need to fret over it. I would just stay with it and know that I was where I should be right "now" and that I was becoming what I wanted to be, accomplishing what I needed to accomplish.

This process works very well, and the more you experience it working, the more confidence you'll have in your ability to shape yourself and your life into whatever you want.

But what if you want to replace an unproductive habit, such as watching too much TV or reacting in a negative way to sharp comments from a coworker, with a desirable habit, one that is more in line with the person you have decided you want to be? How do you stop the momentum of an old habit? To help us with this, we can use a technique called a trigger. For our purposes here, a trigger is a device that serves to start the creation process of the new habit. It's sort of a wake-up call, a whistle blow or a bell ring, that alerts you that you are in a situation where you want to replace your previous response with this new one that you have chosen. One of the functions of a trigger is to stop the flow of your emotional response to a situation and bring you into a present-moment, nonjudgmental posture so that you can be in control of your actions. The trigger jolts you into awareness and reminds you it's time to commit to the process you have already decided upon. The trigger is a very simple signal to yourself.

To give an example of a trigger in sports, I work with a lot of junior golfers, many of whom play in weekly tournaments. Before we identify a trigger, we first create what is known as a preshot routine. Its main purpose is to increase their shot consistency by keeping them separate from the emotions of the situation, such as "I need to hit a good shot here or I'll lose the match," or "I can't believe I missed that putt on the last hole. I hope I don't miss the next one." The preshot routine shapes a stressful situation into a comfortable, objective one in which the golfer says, "This is what I need to do, so here I go." That's it; no big deal.

In the preshot routine, the golfers first gather data about what they want to accomplish. This is done very academically, away from the ball and ideally with no emotions. The golfers discuss which goals they want to reach, and how they can accomplish them. If you've ever watched professional golf on TV, you've seen this discussion occurring between players and their caddies, but in the junior golf world, generally, there are no caddies, and the discussion is a dialogue each golfer holds with herself. Let's apply this to our workplace scenario mentioned earlier. Say to yourself, "Every time my coworker makes an irritating remark, I tend to react in a negative way, and this is not serving me well. So when this situation occurs again, I need to take a different action."

This new action is the one that you want to habitualize. We must acknowledge here that emotionally laden encounters are among the most challenging ones in which to create new habits of response, because the old habits we want to change arise out of the emotions we immediately experience. Those emotions will still exist no matter what we do, so we need to get out ahead of them, if possible, so that we can consciously choose what to do next. Golfers actually practice preshot routines on their own over and over again until the routines are so natural and comfortable that they become a place to mentally retreat when the golfers feel they are in very stressful positions.

You can create a "preshot" routine that functions in the same way for our workplace scenario, too. You decide on the reaction you want to execute in the safety and unemotional state of a nonjudgmental frame of mind. In that state, you are fully objective and make choices and decisions without mental or emotional clutter. As with the golfer, it is not a bad idea to practice your response: Imagine your coworker barking at you for no reason or saying something that is totally uncalled for. Now envision him in your mind as having no power over you. Observe him with almost detached amusement as you calmly decide how you will respond.

However, as I said, we still need our trigger. It will enable us to start the routines we have so craftily designed and practiced. Such is the case for the golfers. They can gather data and make decisions, but sooner or later they have to step into the playing box, where it all counts. They still have to hit the shot. This is where the trigger comes in. It's a simple movement that reminds the golfer to start the routine. It could be said it serves to say "let's get this party started." If you watch carefully for triggers, you will see golfers' subtle motions, such as tugging on the shoulders of their shirts, pulling on their earlobes, or spinning the golf club in their hands. These are all examples of the trigger for that golfer that says "my routine starts *now*."

Let's return to the workplace and find a trigger that, as I said, lets you get out ahead of your emotions so you can .execute the response you have decided upon and thereby begin to make that response your new habitual reaction to the problem coworker. With difficult people, it can be easy to find a trigger: the person merely enters your presence. Once he makes an unpleasant remark, try to use that very first pop of emotion — your sense of offense or annoyance — as your trigger. It is very comforting to know that when you remain present in an effort like this, and when you have a predetermined intention about how to react, that intention will, with surprising quickness, come to your rescue and give you that little edge in personal control you need to stay ahead of your reaction. Then your new reaction becomes self-perpetuating. You execute the reaction you want; then your internal reaction to your response feels good because you have protected your inner peace, and you experience the paycheck for your effort. This gives you the emotional and mental stamina to stay with your effort. Thus a new habit begins to form. Eventually the whole process begins to fade into the background as it becomes a natural part of who you are and how you process a situation.

If you were trying to replace the habit of plopping in front of the TV for two hours with reading a good book or taking a walk, the act of picking up the remote could be a good trigger that stops the process and shifts you into your new routine of thinking, "Oops, here comes that impulse to invest time in watching something that really isn't going to improve my mood."

Being aware that all your motions, be they physical or mental, are habits and that you have the power to choose which habits you will create is very liberating. *You* are in control. Remember also that if you start to experience an emotion such as frustration, you have fallen out of the process. You are back in the false sense of thinking, "There is some place other than where I actually am now that I need to be. Only then will I be happy." This is totally untrue and counterproductive. To the contrary, you are exactly where you should be right now. You are a flower.

*All the patience you will ever need
is already within you.*

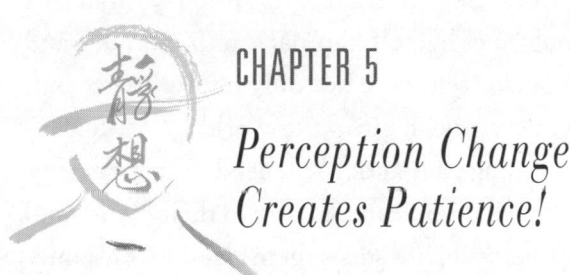

CHAPTER 5

Perception Change Creates Patience!

My mother, who passed on from cancer a number of years ago, once expressed to me an observation she had made about herself as she sorted out both her illness and her situation in her mind. It is worth passing on here.

During the time she was dealing with her illness, she was reading through books that served to both comfort her and make her more aware of her spiritual nature. This daily routine gave her a soothing perspective during what was surely a difficult time. Though she tried to keep up with this routine, there were times when, for whatever reason, she drifted away from both the reading and her thinking about what she had read. She told me one day that when she maintained her effort, her thought process was elevated and more evolved. She felt different about herself and life, and enjoyed increased clarity and perspective about her situation. But she also noticed that when she drifted away from her reading and fell into an "I don't have time" or "I don't feel like it today" frame of mind, she would feel herself slip back into attitudes and perspectives that she felt were not only unproductive but, unfortunately, very prevalent in the world today. Speaking about her reading, she said, "You need to keep reviewing these ideas so that you can hang on to their clarity and perspective. Otherwise, life steals them away." Constantly reviewing new ideas creates, in a sense, a new habit of perceiving and processing our lives, a habit that brings us the sense of clarity we long for every day.

I took something from her words when I was writing this book. There are not that many ideas in this book; just a few, and they have always been there for us to discover. But they slip away from us in our daily lives so easily. They need to be studied over and over again from different angles so that they become a natural part of us. We are practicing learning them right now.

Sometimes I can't read straight through a book because of my schedule. Instead, I might read two chapters today and another one three days from now. I have noticed that when this happens, I often can't remember points made earlier in the book that, when I read them, I felt were very valuable. I wanted my book to be one that you could pick up at any time and open to any page and start reading. I wanted my readers to be able to remember its few ideas without much effort and without the need to flip back through pages to find them. I wanted you to realize that we keep coming back to the same few solutions to all the problems we feel we have, and to begin to understand that life isn't as complicated as we had thought. Changing our experience of life is well within our grasp, but we must review and practice these few ideas again and again so that everyday life doesn't steal them away before they become a natural part of who we are and how we operate. That is why I reiterate certain ideas throughout the book. I also wanted to bring out the interrelationship of these concepts and the interconnections of virtues we all would like to possess.

Patience is a good example of such a virtue. Patience is probably at the top of everyone's list of most sought-after qualities. *Patience* is defined in the dictionary as "quiet perseverance." I agree with that definition, but patience also contains a quality of calmness that marks its outer appearance. I am speaking of patience in general, whether we are dealing with a traffic jam, talking with someone who is having a bad day, or showing ourselves patience as we work at the ideas in this book. Yet why is patience so hard for us to achieve?

It might be easier to approach this question from the angle of impatience, because we all are more familiar with the feeling of being impatient. We notice when we are impatient because we experience negative emotions. When you are patient about something, life just seems fine. There is certainly no anxiety linked to being in a patient state. But when you find yourself impatient about something, your experience is completely different.

Experiencing impatience is one of the first symptoms of not being in the present moment, not doing what you are doing, and not staying process-oriented. Staying in the present moment is one of the hardest lessons to learn. We are always dropping out of the "now" and letting our minds lead us around by the nose to who knows where.

I have observed my mind many times through listening to my internal dialogue. It goes from one totally unrelated discussion to another. It's reminding me to pay a bill, composing a musical piece, solving a problem, thinking of a sharp-witted comeback I should have made yesterday when someone irritated me, and so forth. All this is going on while I am taking a shower in the morning. In that moment, my mind is everywhere but where I really am — in the shower. My mind is anticipating circumstances that haven't happened yet and trying to answer questions that haven't even been asked. We have a name for this: it's called worrying. If you force your mind to stay in the present moment and to stay in the process of what you are doing, I promise you, many of your problems will melt away.

There is a saying: Most of what we worry about never comes to pass. Thinking about a situation before you are in it only scatters your energy. "But," you say, "I have a difficult meeting with someone tomorrow, and I want to have my thoughts together before I get into the situation."

Fine, then take half an hour to sit down in a chair and do nothing else but go through the meeting in your mind and be there completely, doing only that. In the calmness of that detached moment, when you are not emotional, think of what you will say, and anticipate the different combinations of responses the person might make. Decide on your responses and see how they feel to you. Will these responses have the desired effect? Now you are doing nothing else but what you are doing. You are in the present and in the process. You aren't scattering your energy by trying to act out all this in your head while you are eating your lunch or driving to work. This constant inner dialogue, chattering away, brings with it a sense of urgency and impatience because you want to deal with something that hasn't occurred yet. You want to get it done.

The first step toward patience is to become aware of when your internal dialogue is running wild and dragging you with it. If you are not aware of this when it is happening, which is probably most of the time, you are not in control. Your imagination takes you from one circumstance to another, and your different emotions just fire off inside you as you react to each problem your mind visits. To free yourself from this endless and exhausting cycle, you must step back and notice the real you, the Observer who just quietly watches all this drama as it unfolds. As you practice staying in the present, you will become more aware of the difference between the real you and your ego's internal dialogue, without trying to do so. It will happen automatically. Staying in the present and in the process is the first part of the perspective change that creates patience.

The second step in creating patience is understanding and accepting that there is no such thing as reaching a point of perfection in anything. True perfection is both always evolving and always present within you, just like the flower. What you *perceive* as perfect is always relative to where you are in any area of your life. Consider a sailor trying to reach the horizon. It is unreachable. If the sailor sees the horizon as the point he must reach to achieve happiness, he is destined to experience eternal frustration. He works all day at running the boat, navigating, and trimming the sails, and yet by nightfall he is no closer to the horizon than he was at dawn's first light. The only evidence he has of forward motion is the wake left behind the boat. Unseen to him are the vast distances he is really traveling just by keeping the wind in the sails and applying the moment-by-moment effort of running the ship.

Look at the things you feel you need in order to create the perfect life, and think them through in your mind. Perhaps you want more money. Perhaps you believe it will make you happy. That's the biggest falsehood ever perpetuated by humans. When does anyone ever have enough money? The wealthiest people in the world only want more, and they worry about losing what they have. There is absolutely no peace in this way of thinking. The feeling "I'll be happy when X happens" will never bring you anything but discontentment.

There is an endless quality to life. There is always more to be experienced. Deep down, we know this and are glad for it. The problem is that everyday life steals this sense from us. It pulls us away from this perspective, constantly bombarding us with advertisements that all promise to fulfill us through purchases: "Get this, do that, and life will be perfect." But none of this ever works. We need to let go of the futile idea that happiness is out there somewhere, and embrace the infinite growth available to us as a treasure, not as something that we are impatient to overcome.

People involved in the arts come to understand this endless nature through direct experience, which is part of all the arts. That is why I believe that a personal pursuit of some form of art is so important to a person's sense of well-being. It will teach you the true nature of life right up front, if you pay attention.

Getting started in an art form as an adult is not a difficult task, but you need to approach it with the proper perspective. Whether you're learning a musical instrument, painting, archery, or dance, you must first find an instructor who meets your needs. This is a fairly routine task for most of us. We do it for our children all the time. What lies in wait to ambush our enthusiasm is our lack of preparation: We are undertaking an art that is infinite in its potential for growth, and because of that we need to prepare to let go of the goal of being "good" at it quickly. There is no goal to reach other than pursuing the activity.

This is not an easy perspective to function from, because it is so contrary to everything else we do all day. At work, this report needs to be done; that meeting is at 2 PM; and so on. Every task has a beginning, an end point, and closure. We pursue an art form to escape this constant task mentality and to indulge in the total relaxation that flows from the understanding that what we are doing *has* no end. Wherever we are in our process is where we should be.

When I was in my late teens, two incidents changed my perceptions about art and life, and, as a result, created much more patience within me.

The first happened shortly after I had started studying jazz improvisation with perhaps the best jazz pianist in my area. His name was Don. After one of my lessons, Don started playing around on the piano as I was packing up my music. I had never met anyone who played the piano as well as he did. He had earned his ability with years of a solid practice ethic, working at the piano sometimes seven to eight hours a day. While he was playing, Don told me that he felt that if he didn't start working harder, he would never get really good on the piano. I was shocked by his casual remark. I commented that if I could play the piano as well as he could, I would be content to do nothing all day long but listen to myself play.

He looked at me and smiled. "You know, Tom, that is exactly what I said to my teacher years ago when I first heard him play." Don had studied with a world-renowned classical and jazz pianist. I had heard recordings of his teacher, who was extremely accomplished. Still, it occurred to me that if someone could reach Don's level of playing ability and still feel unfulfilled, I was going to have to rethink both my motivations for studying the instrument and my need to reach some level of "perfection" in order to become fulfilled.

The second event grew out of the first, and began when I was nineteen years old. I had been studying with Don for just over a year. I was trying to play a certain passage in a piece of music and wasn't having much luck at it. I was frustrated and feeling a bit sorry for myself for not measuring up to my own standards. In my mind, I wasn't progressing fast enough. I decided that I would write down all that I needed to accomplish musically to meet my own criteria for good musicianship. The list included items such as being able to play fluently in certain difficult keys, playing in front of large audiences, and so forth.

Several years later, I was having another difficult session, this time in a small practice room at college late one night. I remember thinking to myself that I was never going to get any better, no matter how hard I tried. Depressed, I decided to quit for the evening. As I started packing up my music, a crumpled slip of paper fell out of one of my music books. It was the five-year music plan I had made when I was nineteen years old. I was twenty-two now, and I had completely forgotten about it. I sat down and began reading the list to myself. What I read took me by surprise and made a lasting impression.

I had accomplished everything on the list in fewer than three years, not five. In fact, I had done things musically that I couldn't even imagine doing when I was nineteen, and yet I didn't feel any different. I didn't feel any happier with my music or any better as a musician. My horizon was moving away from me. My concept of a good musician was coming from a different frame of reference. I had a realization that took several minutes to fully evolve. I became aware that there was no point of musical excellence out there that would free me from the feeling that I needed to get better. I understood that there was no point I could reach where I would feel that I had finally done it, that I was as good as I needed to be, and that there was no need to improve because I had arrived at my goal. It was an epiphany. At first I felt overwhelming depression and fear, but these were immediately followed by joy and relief of the same magnitude. I knew that what I was experiencing was a realization that all true artists must go through. It was the only way to build the stamina necessary to continue in an infinite study.

There was a sense of freedom in knowing that I would never run out of room to grow. There was peace in knowing the race was over. Where I was right now was just where I should be, given the amount of effort I had expended. I saw the wake behind my boat for the first time, and I realized I was moving ahead, and pretty quickly, as a matter of fact. But the most important truth revealed to me in that moment was this: My real joy was found in my ability to learn and to experience my growth, moment by moment. The process of discovering the ability to create music that had always been within me was the goal, and I achieved that goal in every second I was practicing. There were no mistakes being made, just a process of discovering what worked and what didn't. I was no longer struggling up a mountain toward some imaginary musical summit that would make my life complete. I realized the infinite nature of music, and I was relieved instead of intimidated or frustrated.

That moment marked the beginning of my shift in awareness about how I approached anything in life that required applied effort over long periods of time. That subtle shift in perception — and that is all it was — generated unlimited patience with myself. I became patient with my progress. Not only did I stop looking *at* my progress, but I stopped looking *for* my progress altogether. Progress is a natural result of staying focused on the process of doing anything. When you stay on purpose, focused in the present moment, the goal comes *toward* you with frictionless ease. However, when you constantly focus on the goal you are aiming for, you push it away instead of pulling it toward you. In every moment that you look at the goal and compare your position to it, you affirm to yourself that you haven't reached it. In reality, you need to acknowledge the goal to yourself only occasionally, using it as a rudder to keep you moving in the right direction.

It's like swimming across a lake toward a large tree on the other side. You focus on keeping your head down and pulling the water past you with each stroke. You fill your lungs with fresh air and then expel it in a relaxed fashion, glancing at the position of the tree on the distant shore every so often to keep your sense of direction. You do this with total detachment, or at least as much as you can muster. You say to yourself, "Oh, I need to steer a little to the left; that's better." If, however, you try to keep your head above the water the whole time, watching the tree and measuring how much closer you are to it after each stroke and kick, you'll waste enormous amounts of energy. You will become frustrated, exhausted, and impatient. You will become emotional and judgmental about your progress and lose your stamina. All this energy you are wasting could be funneled into reaching the far side of the lake, but instead you are dissipating it through incorrect effort, which produces negative emotions. You are fighting yourself and pushing against the task. It will take you longer to reach the tree, if you reach it at all.

We have seriously missed the boat with this whole concept in our culture. We not only take the opposite path to an extreme but are so infatuated with reaching the goal of our efforts that we miss the point entirely. Here are just two examples that will further illustrate this.

In the early 1970s, you could go to any mall in the

country that had a music store, and you would find a sales-person demonstrating what I call a self-playing organ. These instruments were designed for people who wanted to learn how to play the organ but also wanted to play it right away. They didn't want to spend years of practice to do it. The organ manufacturers saw this as an opportunity, and set about exploiting it by designing a keyboard that tapped into that personality.

In case you were never exposed to one of these cheesy keyboards, they worked like this: Usually, you pushed one key with the left hand and one with the right, and the organ played a full arrangement of the particular song you had selected. The organs came with all the popular music of the day, and oldies, too. That music showed you which note, and I do mean *each* note, to push with each finger to play your favorite song. In short, the keyboard knew how to create the accompaniment for the piece based on which keys you pushed down. You played one note with the right hand, and it created the chords needed to make the song sound as if you had practiced it long and hard. Since you needed only two fingers to play, you could have played entire arrangements with a pair of chopsticks.

Did these organs sell? Certainly. People loved the idea of impressing their unknowing friends with how well they could suddenly play. The salespeople who demonstrated them could truly play, though that wasn't normally discussed, even when they added a few extra notes here and there. Even if customers noticed, they wanted to believe they could play instantly, so they ignored it. They would push one note here, another there, and the organ would produce a performance equivalent to, say, that of an intermediate student. The whole time they would exclaim, "I can really play." "No, you can't," I used to think to myself. "You aren't really playing. The organ is playing, and it's having much more fun than you can ever imagine."

The point here is obvious, but many of us don't see it. Cheating discipline doesn't work. The people who bought these organs, hoping to experience playing, didn't understand that pushing buttons is not the same as playing, and they didn't know that no matter how many buttons they pushed, they still wouldn't know how playing music felt. To express a melody on any instrument as it comes from your heart is an experience you have to earn. The universe is not about to give that away for anything but your personal effort. As you work at the process of learning music, you spend time alone with yourself and the energy of music or whatever art form you pursue. It's a very honorable relationship, really. You need music to express yourself, and music needs you to be expressed. You give your time and energy to music, and it returns the effort a thousandfold. A lot of the joy of expressing yourself musically is in your awareness of how much of your personal energy and stamina it took you to reach your current performance level.

It is fair to assume that we all know this universal law at some level of our being. Whether you are persevering at a diet, exercising regularly, running a marathon, or achieving another personal goal, if your task is completed with little or no effort, it means nothing. That is why these keyboards just fell away from the marketplace. In my piano business, I saw these organs gathering dust in people's living rooms. Not once did I see them being played. That's because the experience of playing them was shallow and boring. What is sad about this is that the people who purchased the keyboards might actually have come to feel that learning to play a musical instrument wasn't as magical as they had once thought.

The second example is one we all know: credit cards. Credit cards, though convenient and certainly necessary at times in the modern world, are a form of instant gratification, but perhaps they should be called *insignificant* gratification. Credit cards allow you to jump to an end result without any effort. You can easily purchase anything you want without having to work or wait for the necessary financial resources that ownership of the object calls for. They even allow you the luxury of excusing yourself for not waiting, as you promise yourself you will pay the bill off when the statement comes at the end of the month. Some people do this, of course, but most do not. That is why you see an ever-rising number of people in trouble with credit card debt they have created for themselves.

Like self-playing keyboards, credit cards give you the feeling that you are cheating patience out of making you wait for something. "I want it now, and I will have it." Handing over the plastic is easy and much more convenient than carrying cash. You may not even be aware that if you don't pay off the debt within the grace period, what you are purchasing will cost you perhaps 18 percent more than its price tag. Long before the bill arrives, the excitement of acquiring the object has worn off. Why? Because it came with no effort.

We are back to that universal truth that just won't go away, so we might as well accept it and use it to enhance our lives instead of pushing against it: The real thrill of acquiring anything, whether it is an object or a personal goal, is your anticipation of the moment of receiving it. The real joy lies in creating and sustaining the stamina and patience needed to work for something over a period of time. Like swimming across the lake toward the large tree, we focus on each moment of our effort toward the object, acknowledging the object to ourselves only occasionally to maintain our energy and direction. When the time to actually acquire it comes, we have generated a tremendous amount of energy. We have earned the privilege to acquire the object, and that acquisition is the culmination of our entire process: the discipline, the work, the restraint, the patience. Finally we hold it in our hands. The reward feels so much larger than when we just get it with a phone call or plunk down a card.

So many people miss this point. They look at the process of working for something as an annoying effort they have to go through to get what they want. They make the thing the goal, instead of the process of getting that thing. Just getting the thing produces a very small return investment of inner joy compared with the dividend gleaned from the process of getting there and achieving the goal. The key word here is *achieving*. *Getting* the goal and *achieving* it are worlds apart. Most people spend their lives on an endless treadmill: they get one thing after another, but they get no experience of lasting joy or personal growth.

To change your perspective, you must first realize this truth, and, second, you must become aware of those times that you are in the process of working toward a particular goal. When you make a decision to acquire something whose acquisition will require a long-term commitment, pick the goal and then be aware that you are entering the process of achieving the goal. You cannot do this if you constantly make the end result your point of focus. You have acknowledged the goal; now let go of it and put your energy into the practice and process that will move you toward that goal.

When you let go of your attachment to the object you desire and make your desire the *experience* of staying focused on working toward that object, you fulfill that desire in every minute that you remain patient with your circumstances. There is no reason not to be patient. There is no effort, no "trying to be patient" here. Patience is just a natural outgrowth of your shifted perspective. This shift in perspective is very small and subtle on the one hand, but it has enormous freeing power. No task seems too large to undertake. Your confidence goes way up, as does your patience with yourself. You are always achieving your goal, and there are no mistakes or time limits to create stress.

To use music as an example once again, suppose you are trying to learn to play a piece of music and you come from this new perspective. Your experience will be totally different than what people usually anticipate when they're learning to play a musical composition. In the old way, you'd feel sure that you would not be happy or "successful" until you could play the piece of music flawlessly. Every wrong note you hit, every moment you spent struggling with the piece, would be an affirmation that you had not reached your goal. If, however, your goal is *learning* to play the piece of music, then the feeling of struggle dissolves away. In each moment you spend putting effort into learning the piece, you are achieving your goal. An incorrect note is just part of learning to play the correct note; it is not a judgment of your playing ability. In each moment you spend with the instrument, you are learning information and gaining energy that will work for you in other pieces of music. Your comprehension of music and the experience of learning it are expanding. All this is happening with no sense of frustration or impatience. What more could you ask for from just a shift in perspective?

Are there any techniques that can help you integrate this mindset into your everyday life? The answer is yes. The next chapters in this book explain techniques I have learned from many areas of life that can help you shift perspective and gain patience. These techniques can be a challenge to our Western minds, but they are simple to understand, and I have tried to define most of them with one or two keywords. I have found that with these keywords, it is much easier to recall the techniques whenever you are involved in frustrating situations. You will find that by reviewing these techniques from time to time, you will better deal with the constant "product, not process" orientation so prevalent in our culture. Let's get to work.

*Simplicity in effort will conquer
the most complex of tasks.*

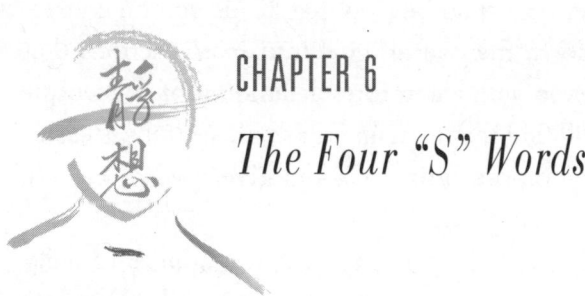

CHAPTER 6

The Four "S" Words

The four "S" words are *simplify*, *small*, *short*, and *slow*. As you will see, these concepts are deeply interrelated and flow back and forth into one another. As you develop control of your practicing mind, it is important to work in a fashion that makes staying in the process as easy as possible, and these four techniques, each one basic and straightforward on its own, can help you do just that.

Simplify. When you work at a specific project or activity, *simplify* it by breaking it down into its component sections. Don't set goals that are too far beyond your reach. Unrealistic goals create frustration and invite failure, which can make you doubt your abilities. The success of attaining each simple goal will generate motivation that propels you along in the process, and you won't suffer the mental fatigue you experience when you bite off more than you can chew.

Small. Be aware of your overall goal, and remember to use it as a rudder or distant beacon that keeps you on course. But break down the overall goal into *small* sections that can be achieved with a comfortable amount of concentration. You will find that focusing on small sections is easier than focusing on the entire task and gives you repeatable success.

Smallness, like the other techniques, applies to daily life in general, not just specific endeavors. It applies just as much to a fitness program as it does to cleaning the garage on Saturday afternoon, or developing a perspective change that affords you more patience. Cleaning the garage is an activity that most would consider worthy of full-scale procrastination. But when it has to be done, step back and examine your feelings toward the job. You will find that you tend to see the necessary work-energy in its entirety. You see the whole task ahead of you, and it looks huge. This viewpoint brings about a lot of judgments and negative emotions. You are full of anticipation as you find yourself saying things like, "There are so many things I have to move. Should I keep this or get rid of it? Will I ever need that thing over there again? The whole garage is a mess, and cleaning it means lots of time, lots of energy, and lots of decisions I don't feel like making after a week of work. I just want to relax." All this internal dialogue has nothing to do with cleaning the garage, and yet it is exhausting you.

You simplify the task greatly when you break it down into small sections: "I am going to start in this corner over here and clean just to the window. That's all. I will not concern myself with the stuff over by the door or up in the rafters. Just this corner right here is all I will contend with." Now you're dealing with a little task that doesn't have the overwhelming qualities of the whole job.

Short. Now you can also bring *short* into the equation: "I'm going to work at cleaning the garage for forty-five minutes a day over the next few days until it is completely clean." You can survive just about anything for forty-five minutes. You have to deal with only one corner of the garage for forty-five minutes, and you'll be done for the day. You look at your watch and walk away from the task at the end of the forty-five minutes, feeling in control and satisfied that your goal of a clean garage is flowing toward you. No frustration is involved. You have simplified the task by breaking it down into small segments and asking yourself to focus for only a short period of time. You are practicing the art of perfect garage cleaning.

Slow. Incorporating *slowness* into your process is a paradox. What I mean by *slow* is that you work at a pace that allows you to pay attention to what you are doing. This pace will differ according to your personality and the task in which you are involved. If you are washing the car, you move the sponge in your hand at a pace slow enough to allow you to observe your actions in detail. This will differ from, say, the slow pace at which you learn a new computer program. If you are aware of what you are doing, then you are probably working at the appropriate pace. The paradox of slowness is that you will find you accomplish the task more quickly and with less effort because you are not wasting energy. Try it and you will see.

Another interesting aspect of deliberate slowness is the way it changes your perception of time's passage. Because all your energy goes into what you are doing, you lose your sense of time.

Putting the Four "S"s to Work

In my piano service business, the demand for my personal skills sometimes far exceeded the hours I could work in a day. I worked many seven-day weeks, and some fourteen- to sixteen-hour days, for long stretches of time. Once, when I had a particularly long day of service ahead of me, I decided I would put all my effort into deliberately working slowly. Working this way might sound counterproductive, but I had been putting way too many hours on the career end of my life's equation, and I was out of balance. I was tired and frustrated. I couldn't get a day off, so going slowly for at least one day seemed rather appealing to me.

I was to start with a concert preparation on a grand piano for a guest soloist of the local symphony. I was to prepare the soloist's piano in the morning, along with a second piano that would be used in the orchestra. Afterward I had service work that extended over two states, and then I had to return to the concert hall that evening to speak with the soloist and check the two pianos once again. The workload was about two and a half times the amount that was considered a full day's schedule in the trade. I use the word *schedule* here because I was on a time schedule: "Be here at 7:30 AM and there by no later than 10 AM," and so forth.

When I started on the first piano, I put all my effort into being slow. I opened my toolbox very slowly. Instead of grabbing a handful of tools and thinking I was thus saving time, I took out each tool one at a time. I placed each tool neatly in position. When I began setting up the piano, I performed each process individually, deliberately trying to work slowly.

Trying to work slowly creates funny feelings. At first, your internal dialogue is howling at you to get going and pick up the pace. It screams at you, "We'll never get this done! You are wasting time!" It reminds you of the whole day's worth of work you have to get done to meet everybody's approval. You can feel anxiety starting to build and emotions floating up to the surface. That is because working slowly goes against every thought system in today's world. However, your ego quickly loses ground to the simplicity of doing one thing at a time and doing it slowly, on purpose. Your ego has no space in which to build stress and work up internal chatter. You can work slowly only if you do it deliberately. Being deliberate requires you to stay in the process, to work in the present moment.

After I finished the first instrument, I even went through the process of packing up my tools with meticulous care, just to walk ten feet away and unpack them slowly, one at a time, to start on the second piano. Usually I would grab two handfuls of as much as I could carry and scurry among the orchestra chairs on stage, trying to save time. Not this day, however. I was determined to carry out my plan to just work slowly. We spend so much time rushing everything we do. Rushing had become so much of a habit that I was amazed at the amount of concentration it took to work slowly on purpose.

I took off my watch so I wouldn't be tempted to look at the time and let that influence my pace. I told myself, "I am doing this for me and for my health, both physical and mental. I have a cell phone, and, if need be, I can call whomever and tell them I am running late, and that's the best I can do."

Into the second piano, I began to realize how wonderful I felt. No nervous stomach, no anticipation of getting through the day, and no tight muscles in my shoulders and neck. Just this relaxed, peaceful, what-a-nice-day-it-is feeling. I would even go so far as to describe it as blissful. Anything you can do in a rushed state is surprisingly easy when you deliberately slow it down. The revelation for me came, however, when I finished the second piano. I very slowly put away my tools one by one, with my attention on every detail. I continued my effort at slowing down as I walked to my truck in a parking garage a block away. I walked very slowly, paying attention to each step. This might sound nuts, but it was an experiment. I was experiencing such an incredible feeling of peacefulness in a situation that usually tensed every muscle in my body that I wanted to see just how far I could push the feeling.

When I got into the truck, its clock radio came on with the turn of my key, and I was dumbfounded. So little time had passed compared to what I had usually spent on the same job in the past that I was sure the clock was incorrect. Keep in mind that I had just repeated a job that I had done for many years. I had set up these pianos together perhaps five or six times a week, so I had a very real concept of the time involved in the project. I pulled my watch out of my pocket. It agreed with the clock radio: I had cut over 40 percent off the usual time. I had tried to work as slowly as possible, and I had been sure I was running an hour late. Yet I had either worked faster (which didn't seem possible, given my attention to slowness) or slowed time down (an interesting thought, but few would buy it). Either way, I was sufficiently motivated to press on with the experiment throughout the remainder of the day. I got so far ahead of schedule that I was afforded the luxury of a civilized meal in a nice restaurant, instead of my usual sandwich in the truck or no lunch at all.

I have repeated these results consistently every time I have worked at being slow and deliberate. I have used this technique in everything from cleaning up the dishes after dinner to monotonous tasks of piano restoration work that I don't particularly enjoy. The only thing that foils me is those times when I lack stamina and find myself drifting between working with slowness and succumbing to the feeling that I must get a task done quickly.

You can see that these four components are all part of the same process. Each one needs and creates the other. When you work slowly, things become simpler. If you want to simplify something, break it down into small parts and work more slowly at each part. Since all four components take effort to develop and maintain, you will have greater success if you break down the time that you apply to working on them into short intervals. You will find it much easier to stay with your effort if you do this.

For example, when I decided to work at slowness during that particularly long day, I didn't tell myself I would do it for the whole day, even though I knew that was the goal. I would say to myself, "Let's just see if I can set my toolbox down, open it, and slowly take out my tools to prepare the first piano." When I had completed that, I would say, "Let's just see if I can tune the middle section of the piano slowly," and so forth. I simplified the whole process by breaking it down into small sections that required me to focus for short periods of time. Working in this fashion kept me succeeding at the task and bit by bit brought the goal of maintaining my present-minded effort for the whole day toward me, without my reaching for it.

An exercise I use to start my day in this mindset is brushing my teeth slowly. This sounds like no big deal until you try to do it every time you brush your teeth. We do so many activities on automatic. We don't realize we are not present in the activity simply because it is so automatic and requires very little thought. Brushing your teeth slowly demands that you pay attention and forces you into the present moment. It is a very practical training exercise for teaching present-moment awareness for several reasons. It doesn't take very long, so it is not so demanding that you lose interest in the exercise or feel it is just too much to accomplish. It's something we all do several times a day out of necessity, which helps to make the slowness mindset into a habit. Finally, when juxtaposed against a stressful, overscheduled day, it gives us the experience of what it feels like to slow ourselves down and be fully present in an activity.

As you work at using these techniques, they will seem difficult at first. That is only because you formed the habit of *not* working this way so long ago, and our culture does not promote this way of going through the day. You are breaking away from everything you have been taught when you start down this path and begin to incorporate this perspective into your way of thinking.

Remember, you can apply these simple rules to any part of your life and to any activity you undertake. As you begin to evolve in this area, the Observer within you will become more and more apparent. You will start to watch yourself going through your daily life; you will become more and more aware of when you are living in the present moment and working in the process, and when you are not. This doesn't mean you will be able to control yourself all the time, though. That tempting mindset comes from slipping back into the "perfection" mindset that states, "Only when I can do this all the time will I have achieved my goal." Accepting that this is a lifetime effort, and that in the beginning your progress may seem almost unnoticeable, is part of the lesson to be learned. Keep thinking of the flower. Regardless of the stage of growth and evolution you are in, in every moment you are perfect at being who you are.

Nonjudgment is the pathway
to a quiet mind!

CHAPTER 7

Equanimity and DOC

*E*quanimity is defined as even-temperedness and calmness. It would certainly seem to be a quality necessary for happiness in life. Equanimity is a virtue worth every effort to develop. How do we work at equanimity? How do we bring this quality into our experience of life, and how do we maintain it?

A sign that someone possesses this virtue is that they are undisturbed by the moment-to-moment ups and downs they experience in daily life. Things just don't seem to bother these people. Why is this? It is because equanimity comes from the art of nonjudgment. Nonjudgment quiets the internal dialogue of our mind.

We judge everything in life, and most of it unconsciously. From the moment we wake up in the morning, we start judging. We even judge what happened while we were asleep: "I had a bad dream" or "I slept great." We judge everything that comes toward us during the day. Every experience, every word that is spoken, is evaluated and judged by filtering it through our opinions and our past experiences. This is necessary. It is how we make all our decisions, whether they are of great importance or relatively insignificant. For example: "I want this cereal for breakfast." This means that I have looked at all the available options for breakfast and made a judgment against everything I don't want this morning. Maybe tomorrow I will make a judgment against cereal in favor of eggs.

Judgment requires the process of evaluation, the process of comparison. This requires a point of relativity, an ideal. As I mentioned earlier in the book, judgments are always based on some preconceived idea of perfection. There is always an imagined ideal item, experience, or circumstance that allows us and even compels us to pass judgment. We compare the present situation either to an imagined ideal situation of the same nature or to a past situation of the same nature. When you are unaware that judgments are happening, they become self-perpetuating, and the "ideal" is always evolving.

If you watch a movie and say, "That was a good movie," you are comparing it either to one or more movies you have seen in the past that you judged as good or bad or to some concept of what an ideal movie is. If you are comparing it to a movie you have seen in the past, ask yourself what made that particular movie good or bad. Your answer is a judgment. Whether you judge the present movie as good or bad, the experience of watching it, evaluating it, and finally judging it will be added to your subconscious concept of the "ideal" movie. This ideal evolves because your perceptions and priorities evolve throughout your lifetime. A movie that seems good when you are thirty years old does not fit the same criteria you used to judge a movie as good when you were seven.

Judgments are necessary for us to function in life, but they have a downside: They are not executed with a detached nature. There is usually some emotion involved, and the amount of emotion is proportional to the perceived importance of the judgment. "The ideal breakfast this morning would be Brand X cereal, but there is none, so I will have eggs instead." This is not a particularly emotional judgment, but you do experience disappointment at some level. "My ideal job would be one right here in town, but another job is open five states away. So I'll take this new job and move my family away from our friends." This is a different story. The emotions in this judgment are much more pronounced because your decision has great impact on your life and the lives of your family members. However, the emotions you experience have nothing to do with executing the decision. Instead, the emotions hinder you from thinking clearly and make you struggle as you work to determine your best choice.

I have a private pilot's license. When you, as a student, are working on your certificate, you are taught to fly the airplane based on procedures and to not allow emotions to enter into your decisions. At some point in your training, the flight instructor will pull the throttle all the way back to nothing, usually when you aren't expecting it, and say, "You just lost your engine. What are you going to do?"

What you are going to do is the procedure you have been taught, the one that you've practiced over and over so that it has become a natural habit. One of my instructors told me that every time I got into the airplane, she wanted me to run through the emergency "engine out" procedure before I did anything else. She also instructed me to make it the last thing I did before exiting the airplane. She said that if I did this, should the situation ever occur in real life, there would be no emotion, no panic, and no extraneous dialogue stealing away precious seconds. I would just make decisions and execute them.

This practice works. The evidence of it can be seen in the heroic emergency landings made by commercial pilots and private pilots alike. I once heard a recording of an amazing conversation between a corporate pilot and air traffic control. The pilot was in heavy fog, and critically needed instruments were failing. He was flying at night between mountains, and being told by the air traffic controller when to turn and which altitude and heading to hold. The pilot could see nothing out of the windows, and one wrong move would spell death in a fiery crash. Though his emotions were probably beating at his mind's door, screaming to be noticed, they had no power over him. He and his copilot were entrenched in practiced procedures, operating in total equanimity. They weren't judging their situation at all, just reacting to it. At that point in time, judging their circumstance would have brought mind-numbing emotions into the situation that could have meant the loss of their lives. The air traffic controller was as process-oriented as the pilot and copilot.

He knew that the pilots' lives depended on his operating clear of emotion. It was an incredible conversation, and one that demonstrated that you are at your best when you are not operating under the influence of emotions and unconscious judgment making.

The emotions attached to a judgment stem from a sense that "this is right, and that is wrong." "This is good, and that is bad." *Right* and *good* make us happy, while *wrong* and *bad* make us upset or sad. We feel that right and good things at least approach the ideal, while wrong and bad things move away from it. We all want to be happy and have ideal lives, but what constitutes right and wrong is neither universal nor constant. When Galileo was jailed four hundred years ago for his observation that the Earth was not the center of the solar system, he was considered a heretic who spoke directly against God. Yet today we realize he was among the few who knew the truth. Instead of being wrong and bad, he turned out to be right and good.

If you were to follow a three-year-old child through his life, periodically asking him for his definition of "the ideal," you would get a different answer at every age. At three, he might just want a particular toy. At the age of ten, he might want a new bike and no school, and at the age of nineteen, a college scholarship and a date with a certain person. By the time he reached thirty, his ideals might be a high-paying job, a family, and a beautiful spouse. When he reached fifty, he might want a new spouse and early retirement. At seventy, he might want to either live fifteen more years or be ten again and back in school so he could fix all the mistakes he made and *then* have an ideal life.

Our concepts of *ideal* and *perfect* are always changing. What we consider good or bad for ourselves doesn't stay the same. Of course, in regard to right or wrong, we are not talking about eternal truths, such as the idea that it is wrong and bad to take someone's life. We are talking about the evaluations and judgments we make unconsciously in every second of our lives that jump-start our emotions and bring us much anxiety and stress.

What can we do about this unproductive habit? How can we escape this perpetual cycle? First we must become aware of exactly when we are involved in the process of judging. Since most of us judge all the time, we don't have to wait long for our first chance to observe ourselves participating in this exhausting act. And then we have a special opportunity: the chance to meet a quiet, nonjudging presence at the heart of all our beings.

We must work at being more *objectively* aware of ourselves. We cannot refine any part of our daily thought processes if we are not separate from those processes. At first, this seems to be a confusing concept to grasp, but with the slightest shift in perception, it becomes clear. If you are aware of anything you are doing, that implies that there are two entities involved: one who is doing something, and one who is aware of or observing you do it. If you are talking to yourself, you probably think you are doing the talking. That seems reasonable enough, but who is listening to you talk to yourself? Who is aware that you are observing the process of an internal dialogue? Who is this second party who is aware that you are aware?

The answer is your true self. The one who is talking

is your ego or personality. The one who is quietly aware is who you really are: the Observer. The more closely you become aligned with the quiet Observer, the less you judge. Your internal dialogue begins to shut down, and you become more detached about the various external stimuli that come at you all day long. You begin to actually view your internal dialogue with an unbiased (and sometimes amused) perspective.

I have had times when my ego is going on and on about something someone said to me that "it" considered "irritating," and yet I remain very separate and unaffected. I feel as if I am invisible in a room, watching someone complain about something that is completely unimportant to me. This feeling also extends into experiences of personal stress, such as job deadlines or financial pressures. I have witnessed my ego rambling on about how I can't finish a job on time. When I am aligned with my true self, the Observer, I find myself aware of the stress that my ego is experiencing, but also unaffected by it. I think, "That's just my ego fretting that it will experience disapproval if I disappoint my client by taking longer than originally anticipated."

When you are aligned with your true self, you are immune to other people's behaviors. When you feel that someone is acting inappropriately toward you, that feeling comes from a judgment of the ego. From the perspective of the Observer, you find yourself just watching *that* person's ego rant and rave while you listen quietly and unaffected.

When you decide to engage your practicing mind in

any activity, you are evoking this alignment with the Observer. The ego is *subjective*. It judges everything, including itself, and it is never content with where it is, what it has, or what it has accomplished. The Observer is *objective*, and it is here in the present moment. It does not judge anything as good or bad. It just sees the circumstance or action as "being." In other words, the circumstance "just is." Thus the Observer is always experiencing tranquility and equanimity.

Whether you are going for a job interview, trying to develop more patience with a difficult person or situation, or learning an art form, alignment with the Observer is tantamount to success and freedom from stress. This alignment assures an objective, no-expectations point of view. This contradicts the ego-driven mentality that one must "be the best," and the thoughts that "nobody cares who comes in second," and "I want it all."

Is there anybody out there who isn't tired of running as fast as they can to grab a mythical brass ring that we all know in our hearts doesn't exist? When a friend or family member falls short of something they considered an important goal, we console them with a detached wisdom that we don't apply to ourselves. Alignment with the Observer brings this detached wisdom to bear on ourselves; it brings us nonjudgment and hence equanimity.

How do we become aligned with the Observer? How do we free ourselves from the confines of our ego? Though there are certainly a number of ways to accomplish this, the most effective method for spontaneously and effortlessly creating this alignment is meditation. Through meditation, awareness arises on its own over time. As you practice meditation, you become more aware of the silent Observer within you. Through your effort, you realize that meditation is a process of quieting the mind and your attachment to the external world by going deeply within yourself.

Meditation is not a religion. It has, however, been a part of virtually all major religions. Throughout time, most major religions have had a history of contemplative processes that deepen the individual's awareness of the God Force, or whatever you choose to call it. There is nothing scary about meditation, either. In fact, if you choose to pursue it, you will find it to be the part of your day that you most look forward to because of the calming sense and clarity it brings into your life.

You can learn to meditate at any age and regardless of your physical condition. I have practiced for over thirty years, and I started out knowing next to nothing about meditation. In the beginning, I more or less felt my way along through my own chosen reading material and classes. Later, I studied in more structured environments and with more experienced people. The benefits of meditation cannot be described; they must be experienced. I recommend it for everyone. There are many books and tapes available to get you started if you are interested (see www.thepracticingmind.com for resources I've created).

With or without meditation, it is necessary to consciously work to shift your alignment toward the Observer. An effective adjunct method to meditation that I use for this purpose is what I call DOC, which stands for

"Do, Observe, Correct." This technique can be applied to any activity in which you try to engage the practicing mind, but because DOC is easiest to grasp when applied to a physical activity such as a sport, we will start with that.

I once read an interview with a coach for the U.S. Olympic archery team. He commented that the biggest problem he faced in coaching the American team was that they were fixated on their scores, or the *result* of their shots. It was as if they were drawing the bow and releasing the arrow only to hit the bull's-eye and earn a good score. This was in contrast to the Asian teams, who, having grown up in different cultures, were consumed in the *process* of properly executing the technique that led up to releasing the shot. Where the arrow hit the target was almost unimportant compared to the motion of drawing the bow correctly and releasing the shot. They viewed the result with an almost detached indifference. For them, the desired goal was a natural result of prioritizing the proper technique of drawing the bow. They operated in a completely different paradigm, and because of it, they were very difficult to beat.

What I want you to understand from this story is that the Asian archers were functioning in the DOC process. They drew the bow, they released the arrow, they observed the result, and then they made corrections for the next shot. They *do*, they *observe*, they *correct*. There is no emotion in any of this. There are no judgments. It is simple and stress-free, and you can't argue with their technique because, for many years, they dominated the sport.

However, go to most U.S. sporting events and you will see that nobody is having any fun unless they are winning. Victory is what we focus on. The players' minds reel with judgments about where they are in relation to the competition, and they experience all the emotions produced by such mental activity. The minds of the Asian archers were quiet, uncomplicated, and free from mental turmoil. The irony was that, when compared to the results-oriented Americans, the Asians were the ones who were winning. Now, U.S. sports psychologists are teaching our athletes to think along similar lines.

This technique of DOC can and does happen in the background, and very naturally at times. Give a basketball player ten shots from anywhere on the court. He will shoot at the target, or do; then he will observe the shot unfold; and finally he will make corrections based on what he observed. DOC happens in the background, without effort. Like the player, we want to make DOC a natural part of how we approach life.

If, for example, you feel you tend to worry too much, then try to apply DOC to your actions. When you notice yourself fretting over something, you have accomplished the *do* portion. Now *observe* the behavior that you want to change. In your observation of yourself worrying, you separate yourself from the act of worrying. Now realize that the emotions you are experiencing have no effect on the problem over which you're fretting. Release yourself from the emotions as best as you can — that is the *correction* portion — and try to look at the problem as an Observer.

When you find yourself falling back into fretting, start the cycle again. Just *do*, *observe*, and *correct*. That's all there is. There is nothing else, no negative emotions or judgments. It's tiring at first. Remember, you are breaking an unwanted habit in how you deal with problems. The old habit put most of your energy into fretting and very little of it into solving the problem. In a short time, the new habit of DOC will be a natural part of how you operate. You are shooting arrows at a target: "Oops, missed that one by aiming too far to the left, that's all. Shoot more to the right." It's a game of sorts, and you are not letting the villain of emotions play in your game. Soon the enjoyment that you experience from staying in the present moment will make hitting the target smack in the middle irrelevant.

Don't confuse evaluating something with judging it. Evaluation comes before the action of passing judgment. You can't judge something if you haven't first evaluated it. You can decide to stop the DOC process after evaluating or observing, before your thoughts turn toward judgment. This is what you are doing in DOC. Your observation is the point at which you evaluate your process. Are you heading toward your goal? No? Then jump immediately to *correct*, and skip the judgment because it has no value in your effort.

As you work at this technique, your ability to detach from the emotional content of a situation grows in strength. It becomes easier to apply this principle to more abstract circumstances, such as personal encounters with difficult people or trying times. At first you must depend on your inner strength and determination to separate from a circumstance long enough to apply the principle of DOC. After that initial instant, the game begins. I usually start by remembering a line from the first *Star Wars* movie: The Imperial fleet starts to fire on Luke, Leia, and the gang. Faced with impossible odds, Han Solo says, "Here's where the fun begins." A line such as this is a great way to interrupt the momentum of your emotions when someone is difficult with you or you find yourself facing a personal challenge.

This really is where the fun begins, because nothing is more satisfying than quieting the squawking voice of your frightened or insulted ego. In those moments, you realize that you really are separate from that angry or fearful voice and that you truly are the captain of your own ship and crew. In time, this process becomes easier. Like everything else you practice, you get better at it. As you practice, you become more aligned with the Observer within you, and time begins to slow down during such incidents. You see them coming toward you rather than finding them on top of you. Your reflexive movement *away* from the emotional reactions you are so accustomed to becomes an intuitive habit.

Once I had booked a significant piano restoration project with a customer that fell through at the last moment. We had discussed the work several months ahead of time and worked out a time slot that suited both of our schedules. About eight weeks before work was to begin, I had blocked out the several weeks that would be necessary for the job. Several days before I was supposed to pick up the work and begin the job, the customer notified me that he had changed his mind and wasn't going to do the work after all. People who are not self-employed are generally unacquainted with the situation I faced then: when you're not working, you're not earning money. This is particularly true in service-type businesses where you operate in piecework format. If you have five calls scheduled for the day and each one should bring in fifty dollars, your day's earnings will start to dissolve very quickly should two of those calls be cancelled. Even if the clients apologize and reschedule, your weekly income has dropped, and there is nothing you can do to affect that. This situation, which involved the partial rebuilding of a vintage grand piano, was an extreme. It was Wednesday, and starting on the following Monday I had no work scheduled for the next two weeks. On top of that, I was out several thousand dollars in planned income. It was not a good time. Immediately my ego kicked into high gear, turning on the anxiety machine and protesting the injustice of it all. This is where the fun began.

The first thing I did was to step back and align with the Observer. Then I defined my DOC cycle for this particular instance. Because I had been working on DOC for some time, I hung up the phone with a deliberate, detached point of view. I expected the whole ego trip of anger and frustration to begin; I could actually see it coming before it was upon me.

My cycle was this: When the anxiety started, I observed and evaluated it. I realized that my ego's sense that the situation was unfair was just a judgment it was making out of fear of income loss. I also realized that the situation just "was as it was," and its value, whether good or bad, was merely an interpretation I could choose to accept or ignore. I corrected by choosing to ignore my ego's sense of this situation as good or bad, fair or unfair. I told myself that the situation was merely part of the ebb and flow of financial energy into and through my life. Some jobs I would get, others I would not, and the jobs that I would get would be satisfying because I could compare them to jobs, such as this one, that I had not received. I focused on staying impartial and dealing with the situation in a detached manner, despite how loudly my ego's internal dialogue protested, "But this is not fair! But this is wrong!" I looked at this as nothing more than a distraction. I would accept this situation as it was, not as how my ego wanted it to be.

In this instance, the DOC cycle was composed of my conscious participation in the whole process: I saw the anger and frustration coming, observed my internal dialogue with detachment, and corrected my reaction to this dialogue. When I completed the DOC cycle in this manner, the anxiety subsided and the internal dialogue quieted. In the beginning, the emotions might return in fifteen minutes, and perhaps I would start to indulge in anxiety, but correcting myself was what I prescribed for the next cycle. I did not judge my performance in this matter as good or bad.

Keeping the impartial-observer perspective is what I would do were I counseling a friend through a similar situation. Staying aware that I had a choice in how I reacted to the feelings was what I strived for. Not falling victim to my personality's conditioned response was my goal. I wanted to consciously make a habit of detaching myself and thereby use my privilege of conscious choice. The periods of returning anxiety steadily decreased in frequency and became less intense as I persevered at the DOC cycle. By the beginning of the next week, they were all but gone. I considered this significant because there was a time in my life when a job's disappearance would have bothered me for weeks, and my fretting would have really affected the quality of my life.

In reality, this setback wasn't going to change my standard of living, no matter how much my ego wanted to argue the contrary. My true self knew that. The income would have been nice, but I really didn't need it to support my family. The whole situation was an inconvenience more than anything else.

During the rest of the week, I focused only on the solution to the problem. By Monday, I had filled those two weeks with work and even had a little time left over to continue work on this book. In retrospect, the loss simplified my life because it allowed me to balance the flow of an overburdened work schedule. The experience increased my knowledge of the value of DOC and how it truly does make life more of an adventure.

I have used DOC in every conceivable difficult situation. If somebody barks at me because he is having a bad day, my inner response is "This is where the fun begins. Let's go." As I said, though, I don't make it my goal to stay perfectly detached and unaffected by other people's behavior or life's ups and downs. That would be counterproductive because I would be substituting one kind of stress for another. I make it my goal to stay in the process of practicing DOC and to be aware enough of my internal monologues to have a chance to use DOC.

Remember that when you start engaging your conscious will in how you handle difficult situations, you have to take it in short intervals, at least in the beginning. Otherwise you get fatigued, and then frustration is a danger.

If you were to decide to take up jogging, you wouldn't go out to run a marathon on the first day. Building up the strength and endurance necessary to deal with the rigors of a race of that magnitude takes time and practice sessions. Likewise, the stamina necessary for self-control is a process that you work at daily. You start with short sessions and allow yourself rest. If you are aware of when you are trying, then that means you are in the present moment and you have already won, regardless of where you appear to be in relation to your personal goals. Your goals will always move away from you. That is the way we keep evolving.

Wisdom is not a by-product of age.
Teach and learn
from all those around you.

CHAPTER 8

Teach and Learn from Children

I f you have children, it is only natural to want to pass on to them what you have learned from both your struggles and your triumphs. We do this in an effort to save our children from having to repeat the learning processes we went through. Ironically, though, in some ways, children are ahead of adults in the way they process their lives and engage the practicing mind. We have much to offer them, but we also have much to learn from them.

When I've tried to pass on real knowledge to my own children, I've found that it is not an easy task. The reason for this is that there is a large difference between children's and adults' perspectives on life. And I do mean our perspectives, not our priorities. I don't think we differ as much as we might think in the latter aspect. Kids basically want a sense of security, lots of free time, and experiences that are fun and free from stress. Do adults want anything different?

Yet we do differ in some areas, such as our concepts of time. When I was a child, I felt that the school day was eternal. Summer vacation seemed to go on for years. Time moved very slowly. If I tell my kids we will go someplace special next week, they whine about having to wait so long. Meanwhile, I am wishing that next week were a month away so that I'd have time to complete all my work before next week gets here. If I tell them to do their homework before they watch TV or get on the computer, they protest that the half an hour of homework will take *forever*.

As adults, we usually feel that life goes too fast. We feel there is too much to do in too little time, and most of us long for the simplicity of our schooldays when we were young. And the older we get, the faster time seems to go. Seasons and years feel as if they are flying by. The time between when we were ten and twenty years old seemed to last a century, and yet the time between, say, thirty and forty feels like two or three years. I am not really sure why this phenomenon occurs, but I have never met an adult who doesn't experience it. It might happen because when you are a child, you are, hopefully, still naive about much of the world's suffering, which we perceive as adults. A child's life doesn't possess the quality of urgency it will take on in adult years.

Time perception is an integral part of the difference

between adults and children. In general, children don't seem to have a sense of where they are going in life. There is today, and that's it. They live in the present moment, but not really by their own choice; it's just how they are. There is a paradox here. What's frustrating as an adult, with regard to teaching them to stay in the present when they are engaged in something that requires perseverance, is that kids can't see the point. Why work at something that requires a long-term commitment, a perception of time outside the present moment? All they know is their perspective as children. They have no concept of what lies ahead. They don't see how discipline and effort can pay such great dividends over time, but we do. This paradox is both their and our strengths and weaknesses in the same instant.

Look at an activity such as piano lessons. Many children can't see the point in practicing because they have no concept of being able to play well and the enjoyment that that would bring to them. That is why *they* get impatient. Why do it? Adults, however, do possess an understanding of the point of practicing, and our impatience stems from the precisely opposite reason. We do have a concept of what it would be like to play well, and that is the very reason that we get impatient. We can't play well enough, soon enough. So, as an adult, try to notice the carefree nature that comes naturally to a child, who lives for and in the present. Try to help children to not lose that nature as they grow up in a world that constantly tries to push it out of them.

To me, the reason to work at all that I have been discussing in this book is obvious. It raises my level of control over my life and allows me to choose a path that is filled with more ups than downs. It makes me live in the present and brings happiness and peace to whatever I do in the ever-present moment. It both makes me aware that I am a conscious choice-maker and empowers me with the privilege to make the choice.

I confess that teaching my daughters about reasons to practice is a learning process that I am far from completing. None of us learn anything except through our own direct experiences. Because of this, I try to teach in two ways. First, I remind my daughters of their past. They might not know where they are going, but they do know where they have been. I can talk about an event that was either a problem or a triumph in their lives and help them to understand which qualities they brought into that event that made it seem so. This helps them to shift into an alignment with the Observer within themselves. Second, I remember that they are most receptive to this conversation when they are not overwhelmed by the emotions that were present during the particular incident. I might talk with them when we're alone in the car and their thought processes won't be interrupted by outside distractions such as the TV or the telephone. I start the conversation with something like, "Hey, remember last week when you got upset about what happened at school?" I might ask them how they feel about it now. This gives me a chance to make them aware of how their emotions affect their perceptions of events. By delaying the discussion of an incident for several days or even a week after it happened, I give them a chance to settle into a more detached perspective, and I give myself a chance to decide how to best manage the discussion.

A while back, pogo sticks became popular again, and my older daughter received one as a gift. She got really good on it in a short time, and you couldn't get her off the thing. Meanwhile, my younger daughter was given a gift certificate to a toy store for her birthday. When I took her to the store to use her certificate, she decided she wanted her own pogo stick. Well, by now the manufacturer's marketing department had gotten involved and was making the pogo sticks look really cool, with a lot of extra plastic fittings, but they were really just the same old pogo sticks. When my younger daughter brought her new pogo stick home...you guessed it. My older daughter protested that hers was very plain and unexciting compared to the new one that my younger daughter had bought. Even though both pogo sticks gave the same experience when you were jumping up and down, my older daughter felt she was missing out.

Here is how I resolved the situation in a way that I felt would make a lasting impression on my older daughter. I told her to give herself two weeks to get over her desire to have a new pogo stick like the one her sister had just bought. I told her, "You can swap with her at times if she wants and just keep jumping up and down for the next two weeks." I told her that it might seem hard to believe, but that the feelings she was experiencing right then were just emotions and that they would pass. I also told her, "If at the end of that time you still feel that you really have to have a pogo stick like hers, I will buy you one for executing such patience."

I knew this was another case of instant gratification, which never provides any lasting pleasure, and I wanted her to get past the emotion of the moment. About a week into the two-week period, they both had had more than enough of jumping up and down on pogo sticks. Both pogo sticks were banished to the garage for retirement. After the allotted time, while riding in the car, I reminded my older daughter of our agreement and asked if she still wanted a new pogo stick. She thanked me and said, "No, you were right. I don't really care about it anymore." I knew at some level that the lesson would stay with her forever.

Another way to pass such concepts on to children is to teach with your actions. I remember a lot of adult behavior from my childhood, and much of it was inappropriate behavior. We can't control the behavior of all the adults our children come in contact with during the day, but it is *our* behavior that has the most impact on them. A parent's behavior helps construct a sense of what works and what doesn't in a child's mind. Actions definitely speak louder than words. When I have a difficult workday, I will tell my kids about it later on, when I feel they are ripe for knowledge about how to cope with hard situations. If I am under stress, I might let them know a little about it so they can see how I cope with it by using my practicing mind. Your kids are always watching you. They're not necessarily doing it consciously, but they're observing you nonetheless. I have seen both my best and my worst qualities come out in my kids. Because of this, I try to be aware of what I silently teach them and to make it count.

Many adults make the mistake of thinking that because someone is younger than they are, they can't possibly learn something from them. This is both an egotistical and an insecure point of view. It reminds me of my earlier comment about how we are so convinced that because we came along later in history, we must be more evolved than people who lived in the distant past. I have met many young people, even children, who are more mature and better thinkers than some adults I know. Kids are dealing with a lot more today than most adults did as children. More is being pushed into their heads at an earlier age. For example, my daughters are doing types of math, such as algebra, several years earlier in their lives than I did when I was in school. Also, listening to children's points of view can be very enlightening because they tend to be more honest and open about how they feel.

My younger daughter was once involved in competitive gymnastics. As parents, we always come from the perspective that such activities should be fun things in our kids' lives, not another stress factor. However, as my daughter progressed through the competitive levels, the demands on her body and her time grew considerably. Three days a week, she came home from school and had only about an hour to just sit. She would start on homework and have a snack. She then went to the gym until 9 PM, and came home about a half hour later. After eating a late dinner, she would at times do schoolwork until almost 11 PM and then go to bed, only to be awakened at 6:15 AM, with only forty-five minutes to get ready for school, and start the cycle over again. All this at the age of twelve. I felt it was way too much, but initially she felt it was what she wanted. Several months into the school year, though, she confided in me that she felt she never got time to just "sit still." She said, "All I do is rush from one thing to the next. I never have time to stop."

These moments offer a perfect opportunity to both teach and learn from your children. Listen to what they are noticing about how they are living their lives. As you talk to them about real priorities, good perspective, and engaging their practicing minds, you are also reviewing lessons for yourself. Are you following the same advice you are giving to them? Are you teaching them that you hold the same priorities for yourself? On more than one occasion when I have been overworked, I have talked to my daughters about the importance of balance in life and how at times priorities need to be readjusted to maintain that balance. Children have much to offer because we can learn from them if we listen to ourselves as we teach them.

With deliberate and repeated effort,
progress is inevitable.

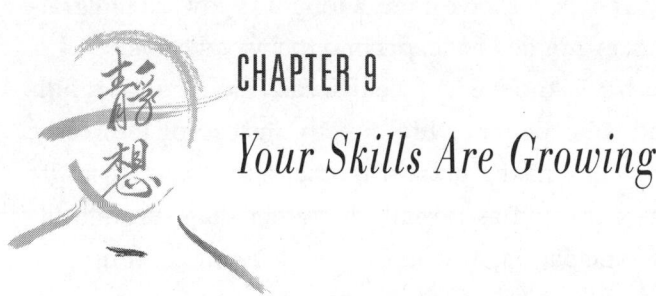

CHAPTER 9

Your Skills Are Growing

In every moment of your life, your skills are growing. The question is, in which direction? What I have presented in this book is not new knowledge by any means. It is centuries old and is relearned by each new generation. When we understand how we work, and when we stay in harmony with that knowledge, we feel a sense of control, and we can sit back and enjoy the experience of life flowing past us with ease.

This knowledge commands us to stay in the present moment, which brings awareness to all that we do. This awareness gives us the opportunity to take control of the choices we make. It teaches us to stay focused on the process and use our goals as stars to guide our course. When we make staying focused on the process our real goal, we experience a sense of success in every moment. Even when we feel we have fallen out of our focus on the process, the fact that we are aware of the fall means that we have come back into the present moment. It means that in this awareness, we have come a long way toward integrating present-minded concepts into the way we live.

With this knowledge, we live each moment to its fullest, and we experience life directly instead of indirectly. When we are in the present moment, we experience life as it happens and as it really is, rather than through filters of anticipation, as when we think about the future, or through filters of analysis, as when we linger in the past. Most of us spend very little time in the present moment. We usually are either thinking about something that has not yet happened (and may never happen) or reliving something that already has. We waste each moment's opportunity to experience what is real by focusing on what is not.

We have discussed a number of techniques to help us develop present-minded skills and to make the work that is needed to develop the present mind as easy as possible. As you begin to use these techniques in different areas of your life, you will, no doubt, experience moments of frustration. These are, however, just the result of holding imaginary ideals of how quickly you should master any new endeavor that you undertake. We are taught this crippling mindset by almost every aspect of our culture, from the educational system, with its grades, to the marketing media, with its unreachable ideals. Everyone wants to be number one, to have the best, to be an A student. This mindset can be unlearned, though, and we must take on this challenge if we are to achieve any real happiness in life. Remember, this mindset is nothing more than a habit. Through our efforts, we can make present-mindedness into a new habit that is much more conducive to our overall well-being. We make and reinforce habits in every moment of our lives. Our reactions to people and circumstances are nothing more than habits. When our practicing, present minds teach us this truth, we gain the power to choose which traits we will manifest in our personalities. Now is the time to begin.

In closing, I would like to say this: All cultures begin by expending their energy and resources on survival. If a culture survives its infancy, its people eventually pass the point of having to spend all their time focusing on staying alive. They get to a point where they can ask *what's* for dinner, instead of asking *whether* there's dinner. Their days have more free time. It is at this point that the society faces a fork in its road. We have been standing at this fork for quite some time. On one path, you can spend at least a portion of this free time on expanding your spiritual awareness, your knowledge of your true self. The other path leads away from this truth into an endless cycle of meaningless self-indulgence that, at its core, is an attempt to fill the spiritual void that many of us experience in our lives. The spiritual track record of all the great cultures that have come (and, more important, gone) is, unfortunately, not a very good one. We can and must learn from this historical truth.

If you look at most of the things that we make our

daily priorities, you will notice that in times of personal crisis, they seem insignificant. And in these moments, by contrast, things that we usually pay little attention to become everything to us. Our health and the health of our family and friends, and who or what we feel the Creative Force is, become our sole priorities, and the dent in the car and the tight budget last month become trivial concerns. Regardless of your religious beliefs, I hope that you feel that everything of a spiritual nature that you acquire in life will be with you forever. Everything else will not. Houses, jobs, and cars come and go; you, however, are eternal.

With this in mind, take time regularly to review all the things that you have acquired in your life, all the way back to your childhood. You will notice that the toy that meant everything to you when you were a child has no significance at all to you now, although getting it consumed your thoughts at the time. You may also notice that your joy in your memory of that toy is not about the toy itself, but about the simplicity of life back then, a simplicity that was rooted in your unknowing, present-moment living. When you look at all the "things" that you had to have through the years, you begin to see that you don't really care about most of them anymore, certainly not the material ones. Things such as the car or the furniture lose their importance and value to you over time. You may even wonder what you saw in many of those things in the first place.

That moment of realization is a good time to notice if you are repeating the process of struggling to acquire things that you are convinced will end the anguish and emptiness you feel inside. You come into this world with only your true self, and you leave in the same way. Everything that you spiritually acquire expands your true self and becomes part of you forever. We need to get off the self-destructive train that runs on the tracks of instant gratification. All things of lasting and deep value require time and nurturing and come to us only through our own effort.

Most of us are aware of this fact at some level. We just get distracted from it by the contradictory flow of information that washes over us every day. You can eliminate a certain amount of this distraction by carefully choosing what you expose yourself to in the way of media, be it TV, music, or reading material. If it doesn't enrich you, then you don't need it.

Most important, if we make developing our practicing mind our first order of business, then the process of *becoming* will become an adventure, and we will be filled with peace instead of struggle. I have put down here for you what I am learning in my own life, and through my own efforts. I hope that my words will help you in the same way that those before me have helped me by taking the time to put down what they have learned. Remember, none of these truths are new. They are just the eternal lessons that we have learned and relearned over the centuries from those who have questioned and found peace in the answers. This is where the fun begins.

Index

true self, 110–11
TV, 19, 137

U

undisciplined mind, 9–10
urgency, sense of, 79

V

value, 137
victory, 115
video games, 54–55

W

wealth, 80
well-being, 81–82

"what-if's," 58–59
will, 22
winning, 115
wisdom, 122
work, 90
    and prejudgment, 56–57
    vs. recreational activities, 55–56
    and triggers, 71–72
worrying, 78–79, 115–16

Z

Zen, 52

About the Author

Thomas M. Sterner has studied Eastern and Western philosophy and modern sports psychology and trained as a jazz pianist. For more than twenty-five years, he served as the chief concert piano technician for a major performing arts center. He prepared and maintained the concert grand piano for hundreds of world-renowned (and demanding) musicians and symphony conductors, and his typical workday required constant interaction with highly disciplined and focused artists. At the same time, he operated a piano remanufacturing facility, rebuilding vintage pianos to factory-new condition.

Sterner has parlayed what he learned from his profession into a love of practice. He is an accomplished musician, private pilot, student of archery, and avid golfer, and practicing these activities fills his spare time. He has also worked in the sound and video arts fields as a recording engineer, audio and video editor and processor, and composer.

He has produced a radio show about *The Practicing Mind* and continues to teach his techniques to businesspeople and at sports clinics. He lives in Wilmington, Delaware. His website is www.thepracticingmind.com.